Cover design by Bobby Bernshausen

Graphics, video and other content references included in this book fall under the Fair Use Exemption of The Copyright Act of 1976, Section 107.

"COVID-19 Human Behavior," by Dr. Anthony Napoleon. ISBN 978-1-951985-36-3 (softcover), 978-1-951985-37-0 (hardcover), 978-1-951985-38-7 (eBook). Published 2020 by Virtualbookworm.com Publishing Inc., P.O. Box 9949, College Station, TX 77842, US. © 2020 Dr. Anthony Napoleon. All rights reserved. No part of this publication may be reproduced, stored in a retrieval system, or transmitted in any form or by any means, electronic, mechanical, recording or otherwise, without the prior written permission of Dr. Anthony Napoleon.

Contents

Preface 5
Contagion Dynamics 5
Infection Potential: SARS-CoV-2 8
Involuntary, Voluntary and Deliberative Human Behavior and Disease Transmission 9
Breathing, Coughing, Sneezing and COVID-19 10
The Science of Breathing Cycles, Droplet Infections and Human Behavior 11
Infection Spread and Hand Washing 14
N-95 Respirators, Surgical Masks and Infection Spread 16
The Origins of SARS-CoV-2 and its Place in History 24
Forensic Issues: SARS-CoV-2 36
Wuhan Institute of Virology 42
Dr. Shi Zhengli 47
Politics, The Media Entertainment Complex and The General Public 52
National Security and Pathogen Friendly Public Health Behavior 69
How to Play Russian Roulette with Viruses 72
Back to the Future 106
Summary 111
Epilogue 113
Appendix 131
Index 135

Dedication

To the doctors, nurses and support staff who make hospitals run from the inside out who one and all left the safety of their homes to go to work so that sick people got the help they needed I salute you. To all the brave doctors in China who risked their personal safety to inform the rest of us that this deadly virus was out there I salute you. To police, fire and ambulance personnel who protect the public at great risk to themselves I salute you. Let us work together to make tomorrow a healthier and better place to live for all sentient beings so that the next time we won't have to struggle with so many self-inflicted wounds.

Preface

This book examines the relationship between human behavior and infectious pathogens' spread with a focus upon the COVID-19 pandemic, and in particular community health related behaviors, customs and practices within the United States of America as well as other developed countries. Pandemics in general, and COVID-19 in particular, have gifted those of us living through this experience a once-in-a-lifetime opportunity to examine the most important questions people in search of meaning ask: who, what, when, where, why and how?

The origins of the SARS-CoV-2 virus will be examined in detail, along with a chronicle of how government officials from China, the United States, and various international health agencies reacted when the first signs of this novel virus made its appearance in Chinese hospitals. We will review the attitudes, perceptions and beliefs that precede nominal community health behaviors and investigate a range of attitudes regarding disease origins and transmission held by members of the general public, and their impact upon disease spread. Recommendations for minimally intrusive changes in nominal public health behavior designed to limit the spread of any number of infectious pathogens, including SARS-CoV-2, will be presented.

Contagion Dynamics

An infectious pathogen can spread with breathtaking speed, depending upon the behavior of the target population and the pathogen's efficacy at infecting its host. Notwithstanding the potency of a pathogen's inherent infection profile, it is human behavior that will either exacerbate or inhibit a pathogen's ability to spread within a given population. In the instance of novel pathogens for which no vaccines and/or few proven treatments exist, socially responsible human behavior becomes the first line of defense against disease transmission.

Pathogens can easily spread from patient zero to pandemic levels given unrestricted transcontinental travel and nominal hygienic public behavior, which tends to be virus-friendly in the USA. Even in the case of simple geometric infection rate increases, the number of people who can become infected in a short period of time can be overwhelming.[1]

To illustrate this point, try this simple exercise. Enter one multiplied by two, with one representing patient zero, who in turn infects one other person. The act of infecting another person is referred to here as an infection event. For purposes of our exercise, we will have each of these two infected people infect one other person, that is two multiplied by two, which results in four people infected after only two infection events. With each multiplication function of the preceding product, we illustrate the power of geometric infection spread. With just 19 infection events, 524,288 people will have been infected.

Keep in mind that our exercise's common ratio assumption, i.e., geometric expansion model, minimizes the rate of infection based upon what we know empirically about SARS-CoV-2, the Coronavirus (CoV) that causes the disease COVID-19 in the same way the Human Immunodeficiency Virus (HIV) causes Acquired Immune Deficiency Syndrome (AIDS).[2] Based upon empirical data, SARS-CoV-2 has spread exponentially since it infected patient zero.[3]

Let me give you a few examples of empirically derived real-world data that illustrate the exponential expansion infection rates of SARS-CoV-2. COVID19's patient zero infection occurred in or around November of 2019 and lived in or around Wuhan, China. It took three months for the first 100,000 people to become infected, but only 12 days for the next 100,000 people to become infected. Within

---

[1] Geometric distributions involve performing various operations on numbers, such as multiplying a certain number by two continuously. Biological systems rarely adhere to strict geometric sequence infection spread patterns.

[2] The International Committee on Taxonomy of Viruses (ICTV) announced *severe acute respiratory syndrome Coronavirus 2 (SARS-CoV-2)* as the official name of the new virus on 11 February 2020. This name was chosen because the virus is genetically related to the coronavirus responsible for the SARS outbreak of 2003, i.e., SARS-CoV-1.

[3] Geometric distributions involve performing various operations on numbers, such as multiplying a certain number by two continuously. Exponential distributions, on the other hand, involve raising numbers to a certain power.

the first four months, patient zero's infection had spread to include at least six continents.[4] From those data, we can deduce any number of contagion dynamics that implicate human behavior as an exacerbating factor in the virus' spread, notwithstanding SARS-CoV-2's seemingly uncanny ability to easily infect its host.[5]

Before I leave the subject of exponential infection spread, it is important to make note of the fact that the course of a highly infectious disease with the potential to spread exponentially can be significantly impacted by changes in human behavior instituted at the outset, when a potentially deadly pathogen has entered the community. Should the general public adopt en masse responsible public health behaviors that prevent just one person from becoming infected at time zero, then seven days from time zero, a full-blown pandemic can be significantly slowed—or as biostatisticians refer to it, the curve can be dramatically flattened.

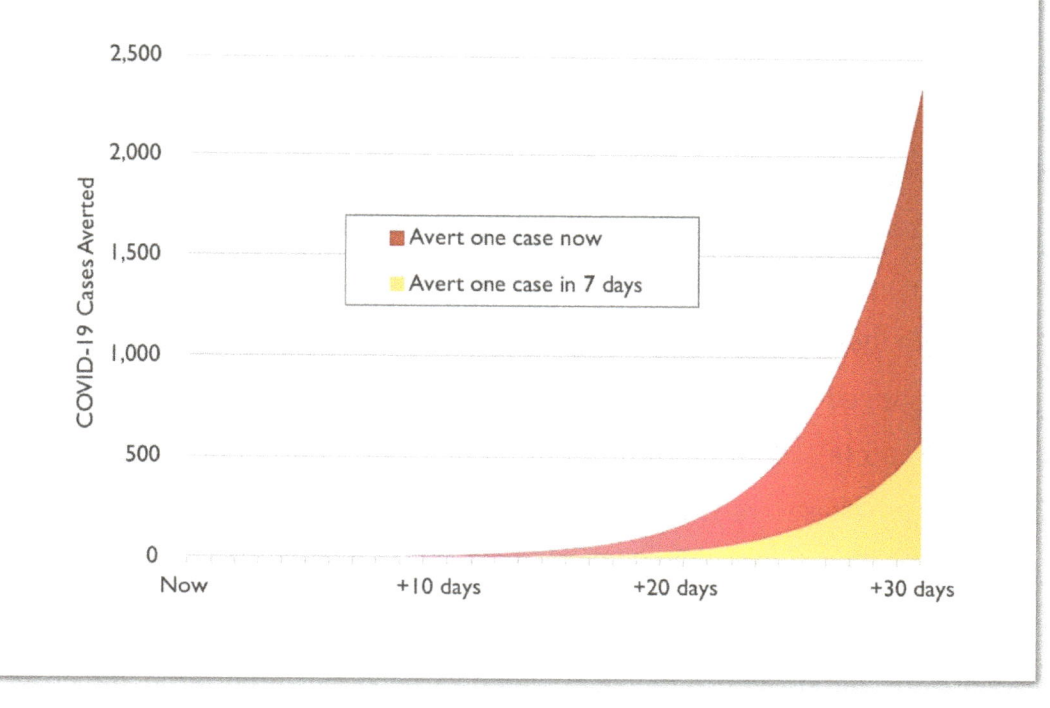

Britta Jewell [6]

---

[4] Johns Hopkins University and Medicine, COVID-19 Data Center: https://coronavirus.jhu.edu Spring of 2020.

[5] Viruses do not possess consciousness. Therefore, when we describe a virus' "uncanny ability," "strategy" or "efficacy" to infect its host, we are using a metaphor.

[6] Britta Jewell is an infectious disease epidemiologist at the MRC Centre for Global Infectious Disease Analysis, Imperial College London, included in the New York Times article (March 13, 2020) *The Exponential Power of Now.* Reported by: By Siobhan Roberts.

Infection Potential: SARS-CoV-2

The World Health Organization (WHO) has estimated that each person infected with SARS-CoV-2 would likely infect 2 to 2.5 people. By comparison, WHO noted that the seasonal flu is spread at a rate of 1.3. However, subsequent research from The Los Alamos National Laboratory estimated that COVID-19 patients are more likely to spread the virus to 5.7 people.[7]

Keeping our focus upon human behavior and its interaction with inherent infection characteristics of various pathogens, SARS-CoV-2 is particularly contagious due to, at least in part, COVID-19's initial symptom presentation. The symptom portrait of the newly infected person is frequently benign. This benign symptom portrait in the newly infected person facilitates the spread of the virus because even people who would otherwise be mindful of spreading their germs to others feel well enough to go about their daily routines without protective measures, simply because they are unaware that they carry a highly infectious virus. Similarly, people who come into contact with newly infected persons are not provided a heads-up cautionary to engage in disease prevention behaviors, because the person they are interacting with looks and acts perfectly healthy.

Any pathogen's infection potential is a function of the number of infectious agents, their route(s), modes of transmission, and stability of the infectious agent outside the host. These are the variables that determine any pathogen's virulence with regard to their epi/pandemic potential. Nevertheless, human behavior, especially nominal public health-related behavior, is often more determinative of a pathogen's eventual spread than the pathogen's in vitro potential at infecting its host.

---

[7] Steven Sanche, Yen Ting Lin, Chonggang Xu, Ethan Romero-Severson, Nick Hengartner, and Ruian Ke. (2020) High Contagiousness and Rapid Spread of Severe Acute Respiratory Syndrome Coronavirus 2. Emerging Infectious Diseases, Volume 26, Number 7, July 2020 (Cited before actual publication date).

Involuntary, Voluntary and Deliberative Human Behavior and Disease Transmission

Nominal breathing is an involuntary behavior, whereas speaking to another person face-to-face is deliberative. Coughing and sneezing are often involuntary behaviors; however, how or where one coughs or sneezes is deliberative. Washing one's hands is deliberative, as is keeping a pathogen-safe distance from others. Greeting customs are deliberative, e.g., shaking hands, bowing, or hugging and kissing.

We know from empirical data that deliberative human behavior accounts for a huge amount of the variance (R^2) in the infection-spread equation when compared to all other variables within that equation, including the pathogen's ability to infect its host. [8] To illustrate the general principal of how behavior is often the most significant factor when it comes to the infection potential of various pathogens known to be highly contagious, let's examine an intuitive case study involving the importance of human behavior and infection incidence involving sexually transmitted diseases (STDs).

The incidence and infection potential of STDs among Catholic nuns is virtually zero, if not absolute zero; whereas STD infection rates among gay and bi-sexual men is highest among an inclusive sampling of demographic groups that engage in sexual behavior. [9] It is human behavior that is dispositive of who and how many people will become infected when compared to other infection modulating

---

[8] To calculate the total variance of any one variable within a grouping of other causal variables, in this case human behaviors as they relate to infection spread, subtract the average actual value from each of the actual values of variables, square the results, and sum them. From there, divide the first sum of errors (explained variance) by the second sum (total variance), subtract the result from one, and you have the R-squared

[9] Centers for Disease Control and Prevention (CDC). (2014, December). Sexually transmitted disease surveillance, 2013. Retrieved from http://www.cdc.gov/std/stats13/surv2013-print.pdf

variables that either stifle or exacerbate the innate infection coefficient of STD pathogens. [10]

Breathing, Coughing, Sneezing and COVID-19

SARS-CoV-2 is a member of a class of viruses that exploit entry points into their hosts known as Angiotensin-converting enzyme 2 receptors (ACE-2). SARS and MERS are similar to SARS-CoV-2 in that all three viruses are variants of a class of viruses known as Coronaviruses (CoVs) and enter their host through contact with mucous membranes. SARS-CoV-2, in particular, possesses an uncanny ability to "unlock" the protective gates that permit entry of the virus into its victim. ACE-2 receptors within mucous membranes in nasal, oral and ocular tissue constitute the vulnerable points of entry for the SARS-CoV-2 virus. [11]

SARS-CoV-2, like other SARS viruses, is classified as a droplet infectious agent. Virus particles that reside within sputum and saliva are propelled outside the body by exhalation events. Virus-laden droplets' physical characteristics fall on a continuum. On one end of the continuum we find visible droplets, and on the other we find virtually invisible aerosolized micro-droplets. Exhalation events also fall on a continuum ranging from the mere act of breathing to a strong sneeze or cough. SARS-CoV-2, as with all other SARS viruses, depends upon man's involuntary, voluntary and deliberative behaviors in order to spread within a given population.

---

[10] AIDS-Human Immunodeficiency Virus (HIV)•Syphilis-Treponema pallidium•Chancoid Haemophilus ducreyi•Hepatitis B•Hepatitis C•Chlamydia-Chlamydiae (a bacterial class whose members are obligate intracellular pathogens)•Gonorrhea-Neisseria gonorrhoea.

[11] Viruses do not possess consciousness. Therefore, when we describe a virus' "uncanny ability" to infect its host we are using a metaphor, not literally describing a conscious agent's premeditated strategies on how to infect its host.

The Science of Breathing Cycles, Droplet Infections and Human Behavior

Nominal public health behavior can either be a friend or foe to contagious pathogens. Hygienic public health behavior, when it becomes nominal behavior, functions as a potent roadblock to infectious pathogen spread. On the other hand, nominal public health behavior that facilitates a pathogen's inherent infection strategies can bring economies to a halt, overwhelm healthcare systems, and result in widespread illness and loss of life. To define what is responsible public health behavior, as it relates to the COVID-19 pandemic, we must acquaint ourselves with how human behavior interfaces with the infection characteristics of SARS-CoV-2. [12]

Humans at *rest* complete 12 to 20 breathing cycles per minute. Over the course of a day, that adds up to 17,000 to 30,000 inhalation and exhalation cycles. One part of the breathing cycle involves the inhalation of ambient air, and potentially its pathogen payload. Inhaled air, laden with aerosolized pathogens (bioaerosols), comes into contact with ACE-2 receptors that reside within the nose and mouth simply through the act of breathing. [13] Exhaled virus-laden droplets that are part of the breathing cycle may fall upon surfaces within the environment. Humans that touch these virus-laden surfaces may transfer pathogens to their hands, then to their ACE-2 receptors located in their nose, mouth or eyes or to any other object, including other people, e.g., shaking hands. [14]

---

[12] Responsible public health behavior based upon what we know about how SARS-CoV-2 spreads provides an excellent template of behaviors that, if adopted by the general public, would prevent any number of illnesses, death and economic losses. When such behaviors are adopted early and en masse in the course of a community infection, they typically result in minimal inconvenience and intrusions upon personal freedoms.

[13] National Research Council. (2020). Rapid Expert Consultation on the Possibility of Bioaerosol Spread of SARS-CoV-2 for the COVID-19 Pandemic (April 1, 2020). Washington, DC: The National Academies Press. https://doi.org/10.17226/25769. "Currently available research supports the possibility that SARS-CoV-2 could be spread via bioaerosols generated directly by patients' exhalation," writes Harvey V. Fineberg from the Standing Committee on Emerging Infectious Diseases and 21st Century Health Threats.

The air volume of the average human cough is approximately ¾ of a liter. Not infrequently, a cough propels air into a typical ambient space that measures several feet from the source of the cough. Approximately 3000 droplets of sputum and/or saliva come flying out of the cougher's mouth at speeds up to and sometimes exceeding 50 miles per hour.

The average human sneeze produces significantly more droplets when compared to a cough, because the act of sneezing involves a stronger diaphragmatic contraction and more of the lung's deeper epithelial tissue when compared to the act of coughing. Approximately 40,000 droplets are jettisoned from the mouth and nose of the sneezer at over 200 miles per hour, five times faster than a cough.

The fluid dynamics of a sneeze tends to produce finer droplets (bioaerosols) that measure approximately 100 microns or less in diameter (approximately the width of a human hair). A single cough or sneeze may contain upwards of two hundred million individual virus particles, depending upon when the cough or sneeze occurred in the natural course of the viral infection. As a generalization, expulsions of air, whether from breathing, coughing or sneezing, contain more virus payload during the earlier stages of the infection than later stages of the disease. [15]

Larger, and thus heavier, droplets fall quickly under the influence of gravity to the nearest available surface. Smaller droplets, especially those that are five microns or less in diameter, can stay airborne almost indefinitely as they float within a sea of moving air. The heavier droplets that originated in an infected person's mucous membranes and landed on a surface—e.g., countertop, tabletop, shelf, buffet protector or bed—may become airborne once again if there is a slight gust of air from a person walking by, a door or window opening, curtains ruffled, or a blanket or sheet moved during the process of making a bed. [16] To learn more about this subject, I have included an excerpt from a New England Journal of Medicine paper on this very subject. This article was published on April 16, 2020, and is entitled: *Aerosol and Surface Stability of SARS-CoV-2 as Compared with SARS-CoV-1.*

---

[15] To better view the bioaerosol mist produced by a sneeze, please view this brief video: https://youtu.be/wnafrAtfMzE

[16] Please see the research of engineer Farouk, Bakhtier on fluid dynamics and viruses to learn more about bioaerosol behavior. https://drexel.edu/engineering/about/faculty-staff/F/farouk-bakhtier/

As a reminder, SARS-CoV-1 was responsible for an epidemic that originated in China in or around 2002. [17] SARS-CoV-2 is similar to SARS-CoV-1; therefore, it provided researchers with an excellent reference model from which to learn about the contagion dynamics of the virus that causes COVID-19, to wit:

> "SARS-CoV-2 remained viable in aerosols throughout the duration of our experiment (3 hours), with a reduction in infectious titer from 103.5 to 102.7 TCID50 per liter of air. This reduction was similar to that observed with SARS-CoV-1, from 104.3 to 103.5 TCID50 per milliliter.
>
> **SARS-CoV-2 was more stable on plastic and stainless steel than on copper and cardboard, and viable virus was detected up to 72 hours after application to these surfaces**, although the virus titer was greatly reduced (from 103.7 to 100.6 TCID50 per milliliter of medium after 72 hours on plastic and from 103.7 to 100.6 TCID50 per milliliter after 48 hours on stainless steel). The stability kinetics of SARS-CoV-1 was similar (from 103.4 to 100.7 TCID50 per milliliter after 72 hours on plastic and from 103.6 to 100.6 TCID50 per milliliter after 48 hours on stainless steel). On copper, no viable SARS-CoV-2 was measured after 4 hours and no viable SARS-CoV-1 was measured after 8 hours. **On cardboard, no viable SARS-CoV-2 was measured after 24 hours and no viable SARS-CoV-1 was measured after 8 hours.**
>
> Both viruses had an exponential decay in virus titer across all experimental conditions, as indicated by a linear decrease in the log10TCID50 per liter of air or milliliter of medium over time (Figure 1B). The half-lives of SARS-CoV-2 and SARS-CoV-1 were similar in aerosols, with median estimates of approximately 1.1 to 1.2 hours and 95% credible intervals of 0.64 to 2.64 for SARS-CoV-2 and 0.78 to 2.43

---

[17] WHO: International Travel and Health. SARS coronavirus (SARS-CoV) – virus identified in 2003. SARS-CoV is thought to be an animal virus from an as-yet-uncertain animal reservoir, perhaps bats, that spread to other animals (civet cats) and first infected humans in the Guangdong province of southern China in 2002.Transmission: An epidemic of SARS affected 26 countries and resulted in more than 8000 cases in 2003. Since then, a small number of cases have occurred as a result of laboratory accidents or, possibly, through animal-to-human transmission (Guangdong, China).

for SARS-CoV-1 (Figure 1C, and Table S1 in the Supplementary Appendix). The half-lives of the two viruses were also similar on copper. On cardboard, the half-life of SARS-CoV-2 was longer than that of SARS-CoV-1. **The longest viability of both viruses was on stainless steel and plastic; the estimated median half-life of SARS-CoV-2 was approximately 5.6 hours on stainless steel and 6.8 hours on plastic.** *Estimated differences in the half-lives of the two viruses were small except for those on cardboard. Individual replicate data were noticeably "noisier" (i.e., there was more variation in the experiment, resulting in a larger standard error) for cardboard than for other surfaces, so we advise caution in interpreting this result.*

We found that the stability of SARS-CoV-2 was similar to that of SARS-CoV-1 under the experimental circumstances tested. This indicates that **differences in the epidemiologic characteristics of these viruses probably arise from other factors, including high viral loads in the upper respiratory tract and the potential for persons infected with SARS-CoV-2 to shed and transmit the virus while asymptomatic. Our results indicate that aerosol and fomite transmission of SARS-CoV-2 is plausible, since the virus can remain viable and infectious in aerosols for hours and on surfaces up to days (depending on the inoculum shed).** *These findings echo those with SARS-CoV-1, in which these forms of transmission were associated with nosocomial spread and super-spreading events, and they provide information for pandemic mitigation efforts."* [18]

Infection Spread and Hand Washing

The simple act of hand washing with soap and water is a deceptively simple but highly effective weapon against SARS viruses, including SARS-CoV-2. Soap is an

---

[18] New England Journal of Medicine (2020) 382:1564-1567. DOI: 10.1056/NEJMc2004973.

interesting compound because it is comprised of two parts—one part hydrophilic, i.e., its polar head binds with water; and the other part hydrophobic, which binds with lipids. The protective membrane of SARS viruses, including the virus responsible for COVID-19, is comprised of lipids. Lipids are made up of long chains of carbon and hydrogen and are non-polar. It is their non-polarity that makes them hydrophobic.

Soap binds with water and fat at the same time, and this fact creates a soapy mechanical tug of war between water and lipids that literally rips apart COVID-19's causal agent's protective lipid membrane. All that is needed to make this happen is the human behavior of washing one's hands for approximately 20 seconds with a fair amount of agitation.

Surgeons have detailed pre-op washing protocols using specific germicidal soaps. This degree of hand washing is not necessary to control the spread of SARS-CoV-2 and one would think, absent an understanding of clinical psychology, that people would simply wash their hands out of common decency and respect—well, not so fast.

Every single adult reading this has witnessed more than one person walk out of a public restroom after a bowel movement without washing their hands. Most of us have witnessed restaurant personnel do this. As a result, according to the Centers for Disease Control (CDC), each year in the United States, E. coli infections cause approximately 265,000 illnesses and about 100 deaths. Over 90 percent of those illnesses and deaths could have been prevented had the human vector simply washed their hands after going to the bathroom, or after handling human and/or other animal feces.

Since humans are literally surrounded by infectious pathogens that have, over the past 100 years, caused millions of serious illnesses, one would think people would do the right thing and wash their hands, not enter public areas when ill, cover their nose and mouth when they cough or sneeze. But they don't and the reasons they don't have to do with education, attitudes, personality, and cultural norms.

N-95 Respirators, Surgical Masks and Infection Spread

During the first two months of the COVID-19 pandemic, public health officials emphasized the washing of hands and, to a lesser degree, the use of facemasks as a means to quell the spread of COVID-19. Downplaying the importance of wearing face protection is out of sync with the empirical data on how face coverings, especially N-95 respirators, mitigate the spread of respiratory viruses. Public health officials not only downplayed the effectiveness of face protection, but they went so far as to state "masks are not helpful" and "may increase the spread of SARS-CoV-2." These patently false declarations require some reading between the lines to fully understand the motive behind such specious declarations.[19]

Volumes of empirical data have clearly demonstrated the value of nose and mouth protection when it comes to mitigating droplet infection spread.[20] Nevertheless, given the shortages of available surgical masks, especially N-95 masks for front line medical personnel, public health officials in the United States obviously felt the need to protect first responders, given a critical shortage of N-95 respirators, by discouraging their use by the general public.

Public health officials chose to dissuade the general public from wearing masks with specious declarations about the effectiveness of respirators' effectiveness, rather than urge the public to do the right thing and make their own face coverings so front line medical personnel could be better protected. However, given what we know about public behavior and the attitudes that precede it, public

---

[19] The notion that if an N-95 mask is not worn properly, it may make matters worse because the "wearer" may be lulled into a false sense of security; is tantamount to arguing that seat belts should not be worn because if you don't wear them properly, the driver is lulled into a false sense of security and may drive recklessly. Proper N-95 use is not rocket science, and even troubled people can learn to wear them properly in less than a minute.

[20] Tom Jefferson, Chris B Del Mar, Liz Dooley, Eliana Ferroni, Lubna A. Al-Ansary, Ghada A. Bawazeer, Mieke L. van Driel, N Sreekumaran Nair, Mark A. Jones, Sarah Thorning, John M Conly. (2011) *Physical interventions to interrupt or reduce the spread of respiratory viruses.* Cochran database of systematic reviews. Issue 7, Article Number: CD006207.

health officials' concerns were well-founded—and sadly, they made the right choice. Why is this so?

Fearful people tend to hoard anything that they believe will afford them protection from whatever it is that frightens them—**their fellow man be damned**. Also, once a device or commodity is identified as important in preventing disease or harm, or offers protection against a threat, opportunistic scam artists corner markets in order to profiteer, to wit:

Brooklyn man arrested for hoarding masks, coughing on FBI agents

"A Brooklyn man claiming to be infected with the coronavirus coughed on FBI agents who were investigating him for hoarding medical supplies, the US Attorney's Office said Monday. Baruch Feldheim, 43, is facing charges of assault and making false statements to the feds on Sunday outside his Borough Park home where he allegedly peddled and stored massive amounts of N95 respirator masks, federal officials said. Feldheim is also accused of price gouging. On March 18, he's suspected of selling a New Jersey doctor about 1,000 of the masks for $12,000, a markup of roughly 700 percent, authorities said. The accused fraudster also directed another doctor to an Irvington, NJ, auto repair shop to pick up another order. There, the doctor reported to investigators that Feldheim was allegedly hoarding enough medical supplies "to outfit an entire hospital." The materials included hand sanitizers, Clorox wipes, chemical cleaning agents and surgical supplies." [21]

The current author is not alone in his belief that reading between the lines is necessary to decipher why public health officials initially downplayed the value of wearing face masks to slow the spread of COVID-19. Dr. Woo-Joo Kim, perhaps South Korea's and certainly one of the world's leading experts on infectious diseases and COVID-19, said this in an interview with journalist Stephen Park on March 30, 2020, at Korea University, Guro Hospital, located in Seoul, Korea.

---

[21] New York Post. *Brooklyn man arrested for hoarding masks, coughing on FBI agents. Article by: Carl Campanile, March 20, 2020.*

Stephen Park: So how effective is wearing a mask in general?

Dr. Kim: It's definitely effective. [A]ccording to research, medical professionals wearing masks have a significantly lower chance of getting infected than those who don't. In the West, like Europe and the U.S., you don't really see people wearing masks. I find that quite odd. The U.S. Surgeon General said people don't need to wear masks and WHO recommended people not to wear masks. But I'd have to disagree...I think the point was to prevent people from hoarding masks because medical professionals need them more. If medical professionals run out of masks, they can't even treat patients, right? In other words, because masks are in short supply in the U.S.. medical professionals should be prioritized.

Stephen Park: When I go outside these days, almost everyone is wearing KF94 respirators (the equivalent of N95 masks in the U.S.). So the bottom line is wearing a mask does help?"

Dr. Kim: Of course it does. Why else would doctors in hospitals wear masks? During the SARS and MERS outbreaks, masks were proven to work.

Stephen Park: Then can we say that because almost everyone in Korea wears a mask, there is less infection in general?

Dr. Kim: Absolutely! If you look at WHO's recommendations, they don't encourage average people to wear masks. I think that is problematic. In Asian countries, because of cultural differences, they do recommend average people to wear masks. Masks have been proven to prevent infection. Just look at China, Hong Kong, Japan and Korea. In Asian countries people wear masks. In the meantime, if you look at Europe and the U.S., the virus is spreading rapidly. ***One of the reasons that Korea has a relatively low rate of infection is because everyone is wearing a mask and washing their hands regularly.***
(Emphasis added)

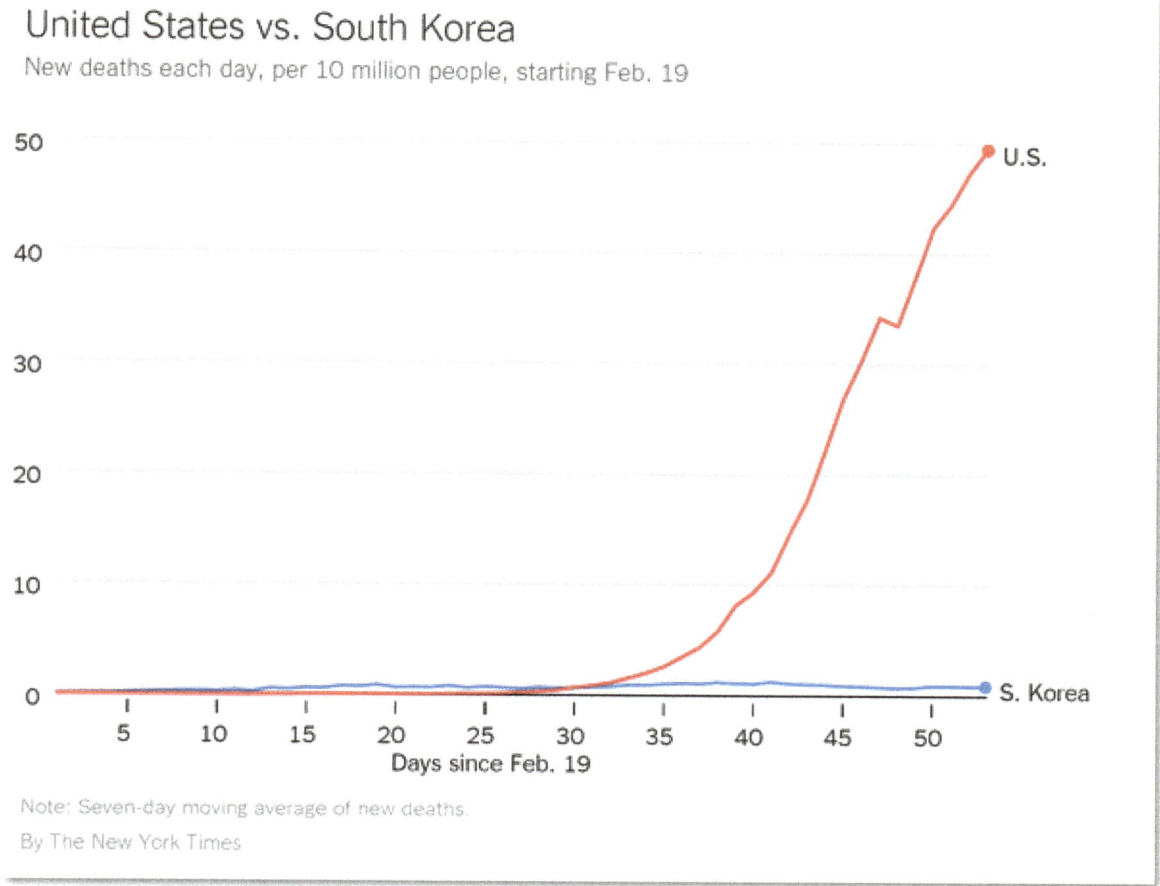

Public Health Behavior Death Rate Data-Comparing the USA and South Korea

Politicians and public health officials who reside in countries where nominal public health behavior is pathogen-aversive have a distinct advantage over countries where nominal public health behavior is pathogen-friendly when it comes to instituting public health policies in response to a novel pathogen like SARS-CoV-2. Perhaps one of the best indicators of this advantage-disadvantage metric can be seen in how public health policies impact unemployment rates when government officials are confronted with a deadly pandemic such as COVID-19.

Take a look at unemployment rates for a sampling of Asian countries where nominal public health behavior includes routinely wearing respirators, social distancing, bowing instead of shaking hands, and an ethos that rejects spitting in public and going out in public when sick.

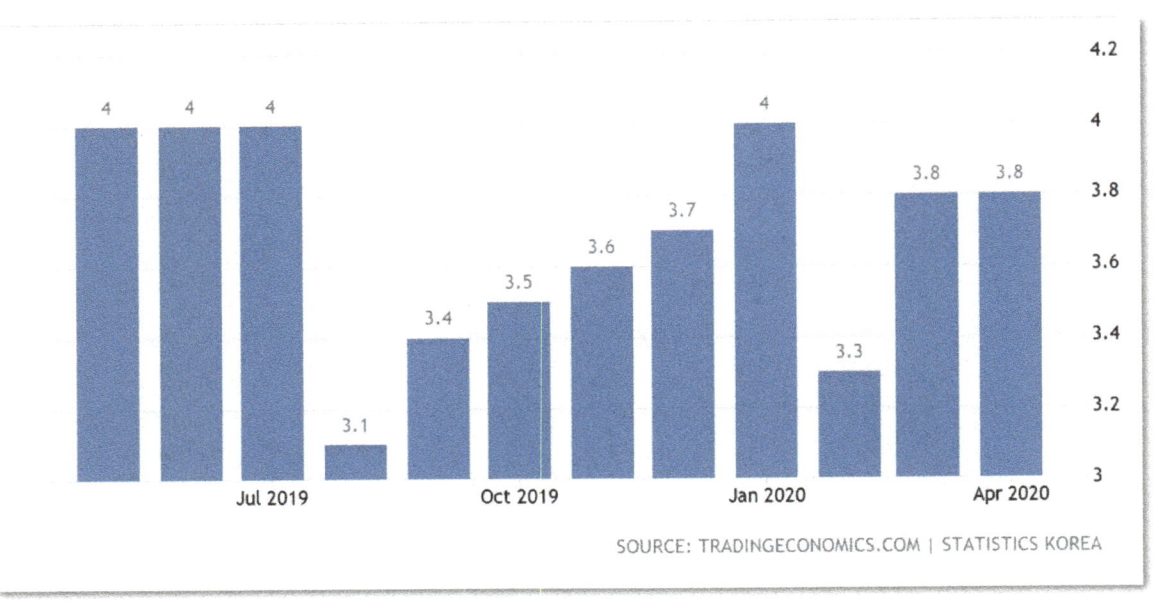

South Korea Unemployment Data

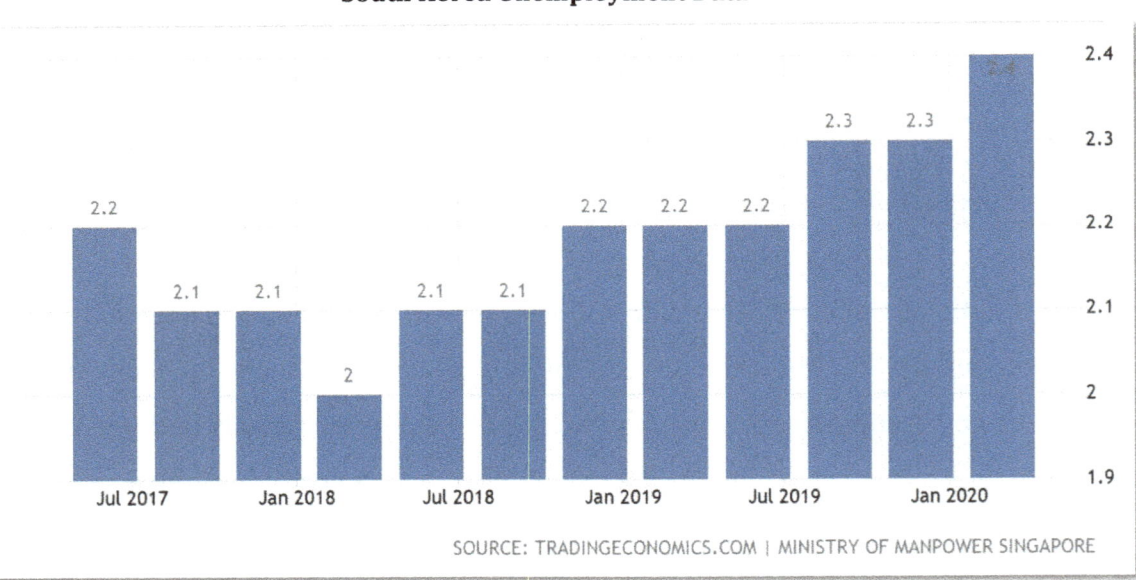

Singapore Unemployment Data

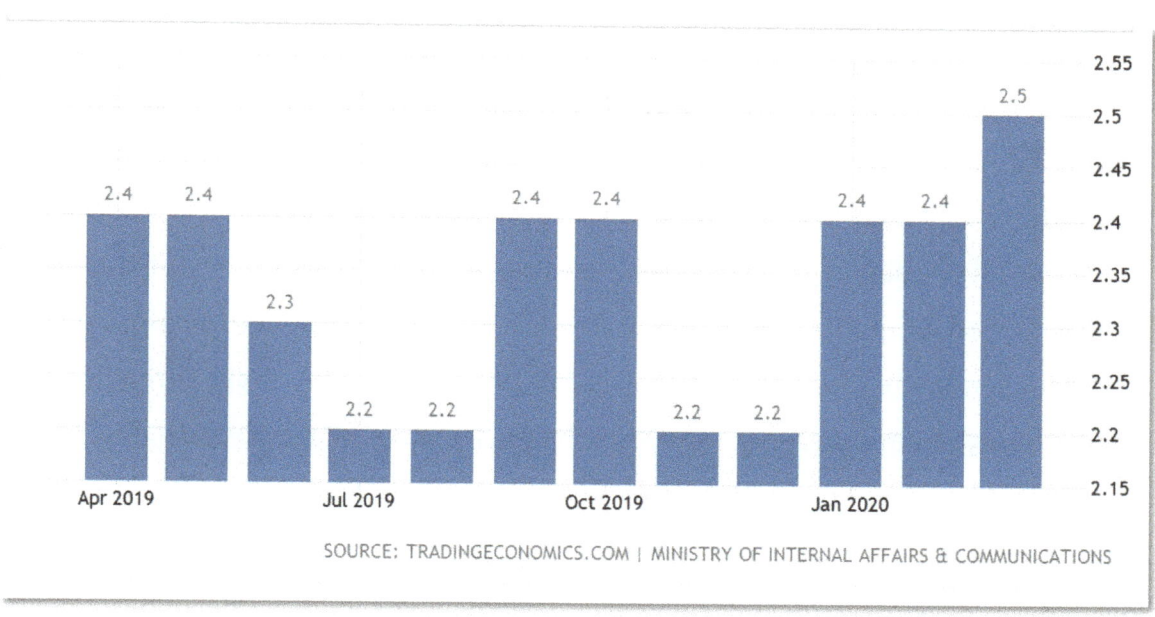

Japan Unemployment Data

Now compare these unemployment data to those in the USA:

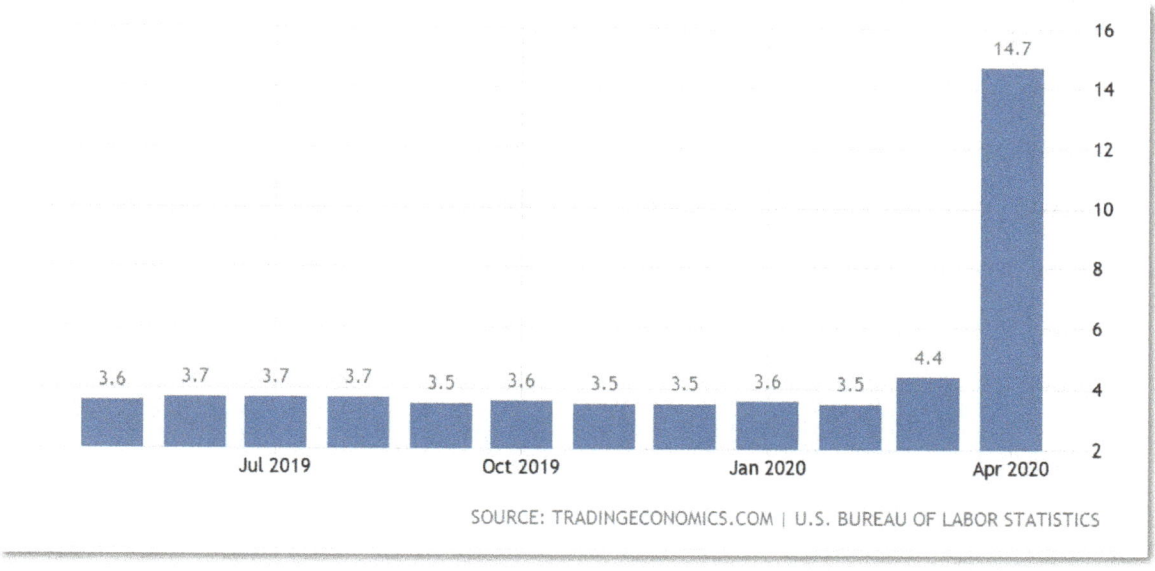

United States of America Unemployment Rate

Nominal public health behavior in South Korea, Singapore and Japan stand in stark contrast to cultural norms in the USA, where people who have a sore throat, runny nose and who cough and sneeze think nothing of spreading their germs without protecting the well-being of others. Spitting on public sidewalks is not uncommon in the USA, but in Singapore you will never see it.[22] The thought of wearing a surgical respirator when you know you have a cold would be unthinkable in the USA and would be sure to garner the wearer lots of stares.[23] Everyone reading this, who is familiar with public health customs in the USA, has experienced obviously ill people try to shake hands with them. Furthermore, if you happened to politely reject an invitation to shake hands with an obviously ill person, you are viewed as impolite, not the person who felt no compunction about spreading their germs by extending their pathogen-rich hand. To make matters worse, the general public in the USA is seemingly oblivious to the incontrovertible fact that **other** people who choose to go out in public when sick without face masks and social distancing actually cause **your** sore throat, runny nose, tummy ache, and in the case of SARS-CoV-2 or seasonal influenza, a trip to the ICU or the morgue.

Politicians' soporific reaction to the relationship between nominal socially *irresponsible* behavior and the high costs of medical insurance, not to mention the costs to the American economy and personal well-being of American citizens, are all part of the same cultural blind spot and/or pathological denial, or simple disregard for their fellow man.

Perhaps one of the best examples of the public health cultural divide between South Korea and other developed Asian nations, when compared to the United States, involves the act of sneezing. All across the USA, people trivialize the link between the spread of pathogens and a sneeze, whereas in South Korea, sneezing in public without face protection is tantamount to an egregious violation of personal responsibility. U.S. citizens in the general vicinity of the sneezer not only seem to be oblivious to the dangers that a sneeze poses to them, but the custom in the USA and other places in the Western world actually congratulate the sneezer with the salutation of "gesundheit" or "bless you." Given what we know about how viruses

---

[22] You will be fined as much as $1,000 USD if you spit in public in Singapore.

[23] Associates of Napoleon Legal Consulting, Inc. were advised to wear N-95 respirators when in public in mid-November of 2019, once we became aware of the presence of a novel coronavirus that had made its appearance in Wuhan, China. Our associates were not only stared at, but members of the general public would not infrequently make snide comments or laugh at them. Those same people who found our associates' behavior odd or fodder for ridicule, five months later, are now REQUIRED to wear respirators.

spread through droplets and fluid dynamics, perhaps a more appropriate response to an unprotected sneeze should be "damn you" and certainly not "bless you." [24]

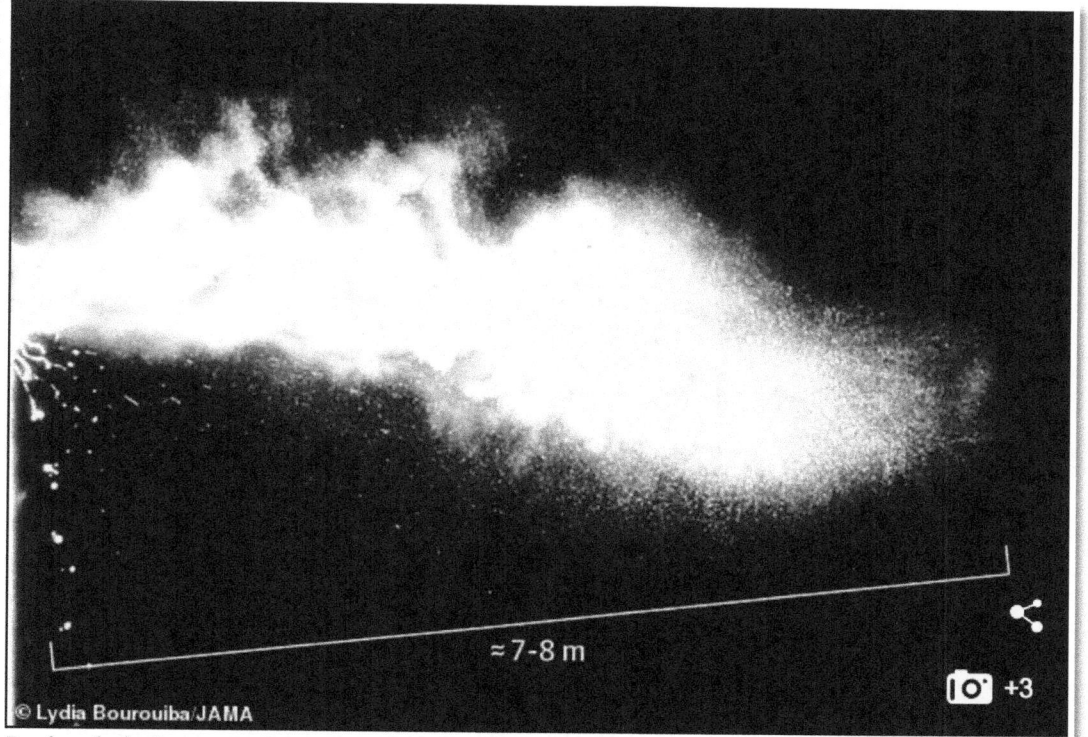

Peak exhalation speeds can reach up to 33 to 100 feet per second, creating a cloud that can span approximately 23 to 27 feet (7-8 metres)

---

[24] Etymologists differ on the origins of the almost perfunctory "bless you" in response to a person who sneezes. Experts agree, however, that at one point in our history, the sneeze was presumed to be related to the expulsion of a demon, the sneezer's soul being forced outside the body, or recognition that a sneezer may be seriously ill and, therefore, may not be long for this world.

With regard to wearing a facemask, the sole focus of the American public, and for that matter the media entertainment complex, [25] *has been and is now* **whether wearing a facemask will protect the wearer** *from becoming infected with SARS-CoV-2. This mindset betrays the fact that for the most part, the American public* **could not care less and is seldom if ever reminded by the media of the fact that wearing a facemask protects others as well as the wearer** *from contracting SARS-CoV-2. Don't forget, from the* **other** *person's perspective,* **you** *are the* **other** *person. Unbridled self-interest has resulted in a public that seems oblivious to the fact that if the norm were to become "be concerned about others contracting your germs," then* **everyone** *would be less likely to get sick.*

The Origins of SARS-CoV-2 and its Place in History

SARS-CoV-2 either mutated from a preceding iteration of itself; that is, changed as a natural process of evolution as viruses have done since time

---

[25] The media entertainment complex includes advertising agencies, PR firms, broadcasters, old-guard publishers, and social media companies.

immemorial, or this particular novel CoV was genetically engineered in whole or in part. A third etiology is what I call cross-pollination, where a mutation originating in nature was taken into a lab, where it was modified, and then somehow re-entered the community in its more virulent form.

From a public health perspective, the origin of SARS-CoV-2 is irrelevant. Faced with a virulent pandemic and absent a vaccine or effective treatment(s), people either modify their public health behavior to be pathogen-aversive, or become passive participants as the virus spreads at will within a population.

People who believe that SARS-CoV-2 was genetically engineered have sometimes used this belief to irrationally call into question public health officials' edicts regarding enforced behavioral changes such as social distancing, self-isolation, and the wearing of respirators. The people who hold these beliefs have, without realizing it, reverse engineered their belief in the deliberate creation of SARS-CoV-2 as a part of a grand scheme to destroy global economies, deny them their Constitutionally protected freedoms, undermine political adversaries, or similar motivations, to justify their resistance to public health guidelines.

While it is certainly not out of the question and, in fact, may be du rigueur that some political ideologues "never let a crisis go to waste," [26] viral pandemics have a mind of their own and therefore should be understood as such. Being able to distinguish between a genuine pandemic caused by a virulent pathogen and the post hoc gaming of that crisis appears to be a distinction lost on most people. But it is a distinction that must be made if people are ever going to be able to discern the true nature of the COVID-19 pandemic.

I want to draw the reader's attention to the fact that long before mankind possessed a working understanding of genomic sequencing, or the technology required to create or modify viruses for nefarious purposes or grand schemes, pathogens in general and viruses in particular demonstrated a remarkable ability to modify their genomes all on their own—which, as the reader can see from the data,

---

[26] Rahm Emmanuel (2008) Direct quote taken from an ABC News interview during the 2008 financial crisis. https://youtu.be/Pb-YuhFWCr4.

has resulted in an ever-increasing number of ever more virulent pathogens, including novel viruses that seemingly come out of nowhere. [27] But it is not just viruses' uncanny ability to mutate to ever more successful virulent versions of themselves that makes them deadly; it is always human behavior that controls the course and character of any infectious pathogen, including the incidence of novel virulent viruses.

What follows is the brilliant research work of Nick LePan and Nick Routley. The stunning graphics that follow come from designer Harrison Schell. *Visual Capitalist* published this work on March 14, 2020.

---

[27] Pathogens, including viruses, do not possess consciousness or develop abilities as in common parlance. In response to natural selection pressures, but mostly because of the sheer numbers of pathogens and incidence of mutations over time, it would be remarkable if pathogens did not develop novel iterations that would, now and then, constitute increased virulence from a human's perspective.

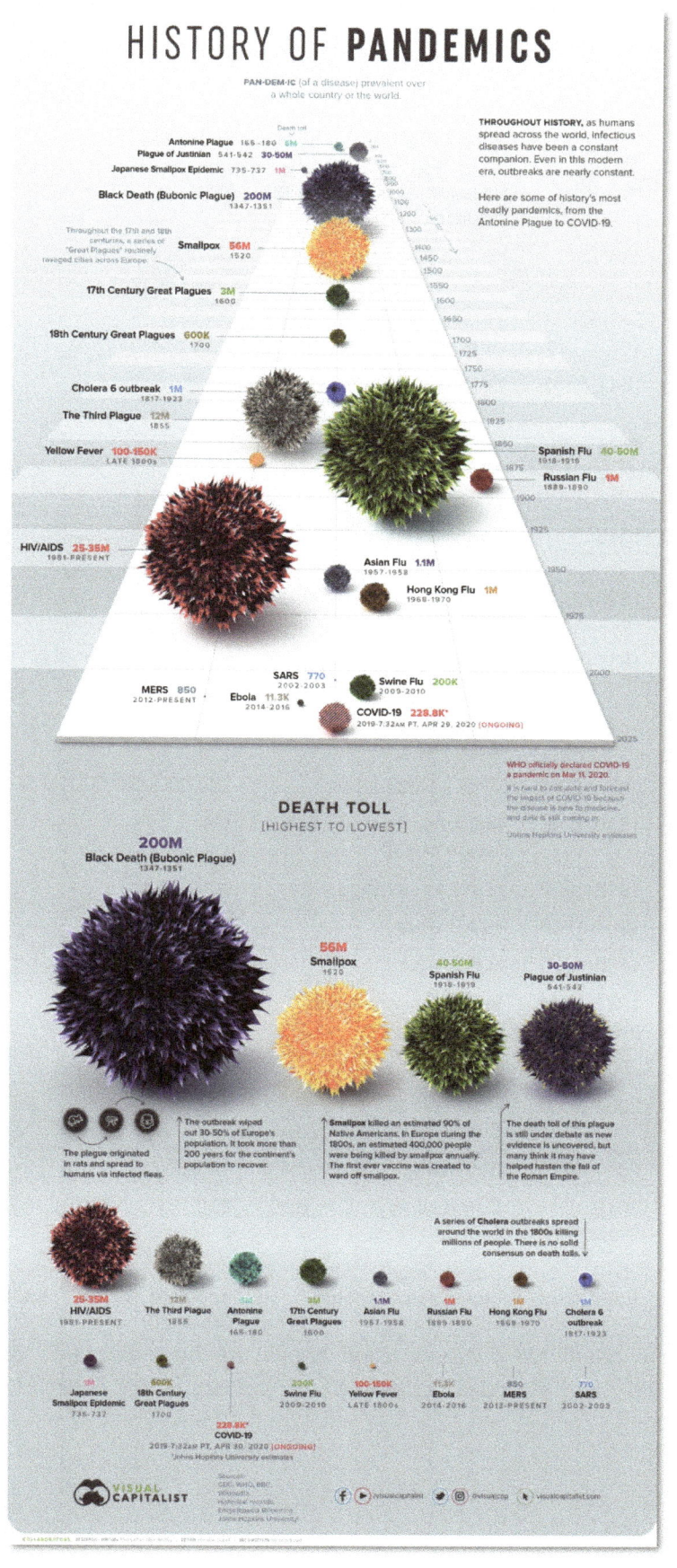

Name	Time period	Type / Pre-human host	Death toll
Antonine Plague	165-180	Believed to be either smallpox or measles	5M
Japanese smallpox epidemic	735-737	Variola major virus	1M
Plague of Justinian	541-542	Yersinia pestis bacteria / Rats, fleas	30-50M
Black Death	1347-1351	Yersinia pestis bacteria / Rats, fleas	200M
New World Smallpox Outbreak	1520 – onwards	Variola major virus	56M
Great Plague of London	1665	Yersinia pestis bacteria / Rats, fleas	100,000
Italian plague	1629-1631	Yersinia pestis bacteria / Rats, fleas	1M
Cholera Pandemics 1-6	1817-1923	V. cholerae bacteria	1M+
Third Plague	1885	Yersinia pestis bacteria / Rats, fleas	12M (China and India)
Yellow Fever	Late 1800s	Virus / Mosquitoes	100,000-150,000 (U.S.)
Russian Flu	1889-1890	Believed to be H2N2 (avian origin)	1M
Spanish Flu	1918-1919	H1N1 virus / Pigs	40-50M
Asian Flu	1957-1958	H2N2 virus	1.1M
Hong Kong Flu	1968-1970	H3N2 virus	1M
HIV/AIDS	1981-present	Virus / Chimpanzees	25-35M
Swine Flu	2009-2010	H1N1 virus / Pigs	200,000
SARS	2002-2003	Coronavirus / Bats, Civets	770
Ebola	2014-2016	Ebolavirus / Wild animals	11,000
MERS	2015-Present	Coronavirus / Bats, camels	850
COVID-19	2019-Present	Coronavirus – Unknown (possibly pangolins)	228,800 (Johns Hopkins University estimate as of 7.32am PT, April 30, 2020)

Note: Many of the death toll numbers listed above are best estimates based on available research. Some, such as the Plague of Justinian and Swine Flu, are subject to debate based on new evidence.

No sooner had humans developed the ability to traverse oceans and barrier landmasses than did they bring with them "their" pathogens, without grand scheme or design in mind. In recent years, destination countries have appeared to care little or nothing about the pathogens that hitch a ride on the backs of travelers from parts of the world with widely diverse herd immunity profiles. Such was not always the case, however. [28] From an infectious disease perspective, viruses should not be afforded civil rights simply because they have infected a person who does have civil rights.

When critical mass numbers of people harbor an infectious novel pathogen, then travel to and/or relocate to a remote country and/or continent whose population has never been exposed to the pathogen they harbor, the destination population's immunity profile, i.e., herd immunity can be significantly impacted. [29] Herd immunity assumes a populations' widespread exposure to the infectious pathogen in question, which resulted in antibodies that protect the herd from the pathogens' ability to infect large numbers of the population; ergo, "herd immunity." The introduction of novel pathogens like SARS-CoV-1, SARS-CoV-2, H1N1, H2N2, H3N3, et al. into unexposed populations may result in epidemics and, if not controlled, pandemics.

Sometimes novel and deadly viruses enter a population without resulting in a pandemic, with the Ebola virus being a textbook example of this. Ebola is such an extremely virulent virus that it kills its victim within days after making its victim extremely sick, so sick that the patient could not travel or interact with others even if they wanted to, save for individuals in their immediate vicinity or those victims allowed to enter non-infected countries for care. Once again, despite the fact that Ebola's initial symptom portrait can make SARS-CoV-2 look like a minor league player, Ebola's effect upon human behavior stopped it from becoming as widespread as the COVID-19 pandemic. Just consider this sobering fact: in Wuhan, China, many people with COVID-19, upon learning that the government was going to

---

[28] AMA Journal of Ethics (2008) Alison Bateman-House, MA, MPH and Amy Fairchild, PhD, MPH. Medical Examination of Immigrants at Ellis Island.
[29] Clinical Infectious Diseases (2011), Paul Fine, Ken Eames, David L. Heymann Herd Immunity: A Rough Guide. Volume 52, Issue 7, 1 April 2011, Pages 911–916.

quarantine them, hopped on airplanes and fled far and wide all over the world, many of them knowingly or unknowingly bringing their viruses with them. Ebola patients didn't need to be quarantined or forced to social distance because they were too sick to get out of bed.

The current author has made note of the fact that many people are quick to arrogantly dismiss the mere notion that virulent pathogens like SARS-CoV-2 may have been engineered and/or escaped from a lab because of mal- or misfeasance, as if we have no record of this happening in the past involving other pathogens. These often times smug and dismissive people represent the other side of the same coin from the people who see boogiemen everywhere, while the dismissive people I am referencing here make Pollyanna look like an FBI interrogator.

Experts in germ warfare and virology don't find it so easy to dismiss such concerns. In fact many researchers have questioned the cost/benefit of creating virulent strains of whole viruses or parts thereof out of the fear that these creations could escape the confines of their creator's lab, based upon past lapses in security. [30] Such fears and concerns are not unreasonable given what we know about this subject, to wit:

The 1977 H1N1 human influenza pandemic

Due to lab mishandling, a strain of the H1N1 influenza managed to escape from a Chinese facility that was likely trying to create a vaccine for the disease. The virus spread globally and had an infection rate of 20% to 70% among those exposed. Luckily, the strain of the virus caused only mild disease and few fatalities.

Smallpox outbreaks in Great Britain

From 1963 to 1978, there were three smallpox escapes from two different laboratories. All three were due to poor standards and bad practices within the labs. Three cases and at least 80 deaths were linked to the outbreaks.

---

[30] Ibid.

The 1995 Venezuelan equine encephalitis (VEE) outbreak

In 1995, 10,000 people in Venezuela and 75,000 people in Colombia fell ill with a VEE strain that had escaped from a lab. The outbreak caused upwards of 311 deaths and 3,000 cases of neurological complications.

Various SARS outbreaks

Severe Acute Respiratory Syndrome (SARS) was a global epidemic in 2003 that caused 8,000 infections and 774 deaths across 29 countries. Since the original epidemic, there have been six escapes of the virus from laboratories — four in Beijing, and an additional one each in Singapore and Taiwan.

The 2007 Foot and Mouth Disease (FMD) outbreak in the UK

FMD is a highly transmissible disease that infects cloven-hoofed animals. Outbreaks of the disease can cause billions of dollars in economic damage, as millions of animals may need to be culled to limit the disease's spread. In 2007, 278 animals in the UK became infected with FMD after the virus escaped from a biosafety lab four kilometers away. The outbreak required 1,578 animals to be culled and cost an estimated 200 million pounds. [31]

Humans engineer whole or parts of viruses in order to develop vaccines or other treatments, and sometimes to add their creations to or improve an armamentarium as part of a germ warfare program.[32] Sometimes virologists engineer nucleotide sequences without the specific intent to create a novel pathogen. And in recent times, people engineer viruses as part of a business venture.

In 2002 Dr. Eckard Wimmer, an expert in molecular genetics and microbiology at The State University of New York at Stony Brook, recreated in his lab the Polio virus, which caused the scourge known as poliomyelitis not so long ago

---

[31] Bulletin of the Atomic Scientists (March 14, 2014) *Threatened pandemics and laboratory escapes: Self-fulfilling prophecies*, by Martin Furmanski, in Business Insider, July 15, 2014.
[32] Germ warfare is not very well understood by the general public. Even those who consider themselves to be acquainted with the subject paint their discernment with a broad brush. The mental image of a virulent pathogen released in the air or water is only the tip of the iceberg.

that killed and / or severely disabled hundreds of thousands of people. During its height in the United States, scenes like this were not uncommon:

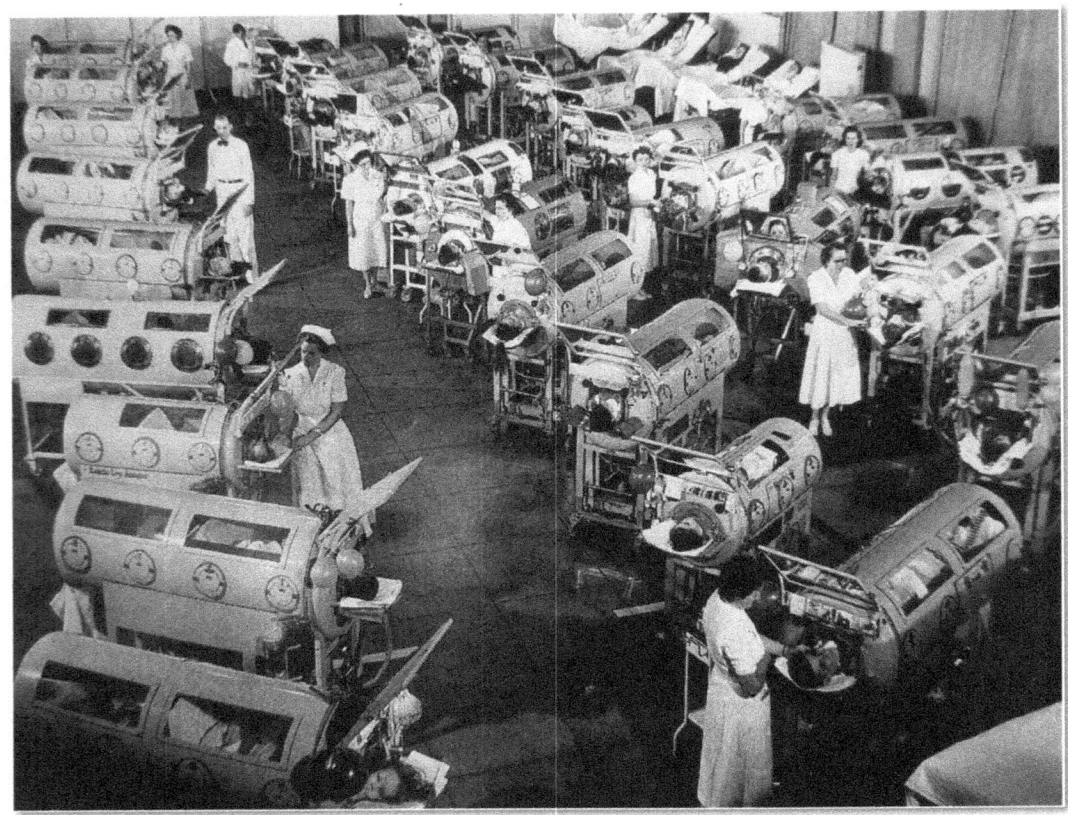

Patients in Iron Lungs due to Poliomyelitis Induced Paralysis (1952) [33]

> *Dr. Wimmer and team's creation of the Polio virus was **financed by the Pentagon as part of a program to develop biowarfare countermeasures**.* [34]

What some readers may find to be shocking is that Dr. Wimmer and team constructed the virus using nucleic acid building blocks readily available for purchase online. In 2020, the building blocks that make up CoVs, of which SARS-CoV-2 is one, are also readily available for sale on the Internet, to wit:

---

[33] Smallman-Raynor, M., & Cliff, A. (2006) Poliomyelitis (1st ed.). Oxford: Oxford University Press, Page 61.

[34] The current author does not question that Dr. Wimmer's and the Pentagon's focus was on germ warfare countermeasures. Nevertheless, the difference between a measure and countermeasure is philosophical and is a difference without distinction.

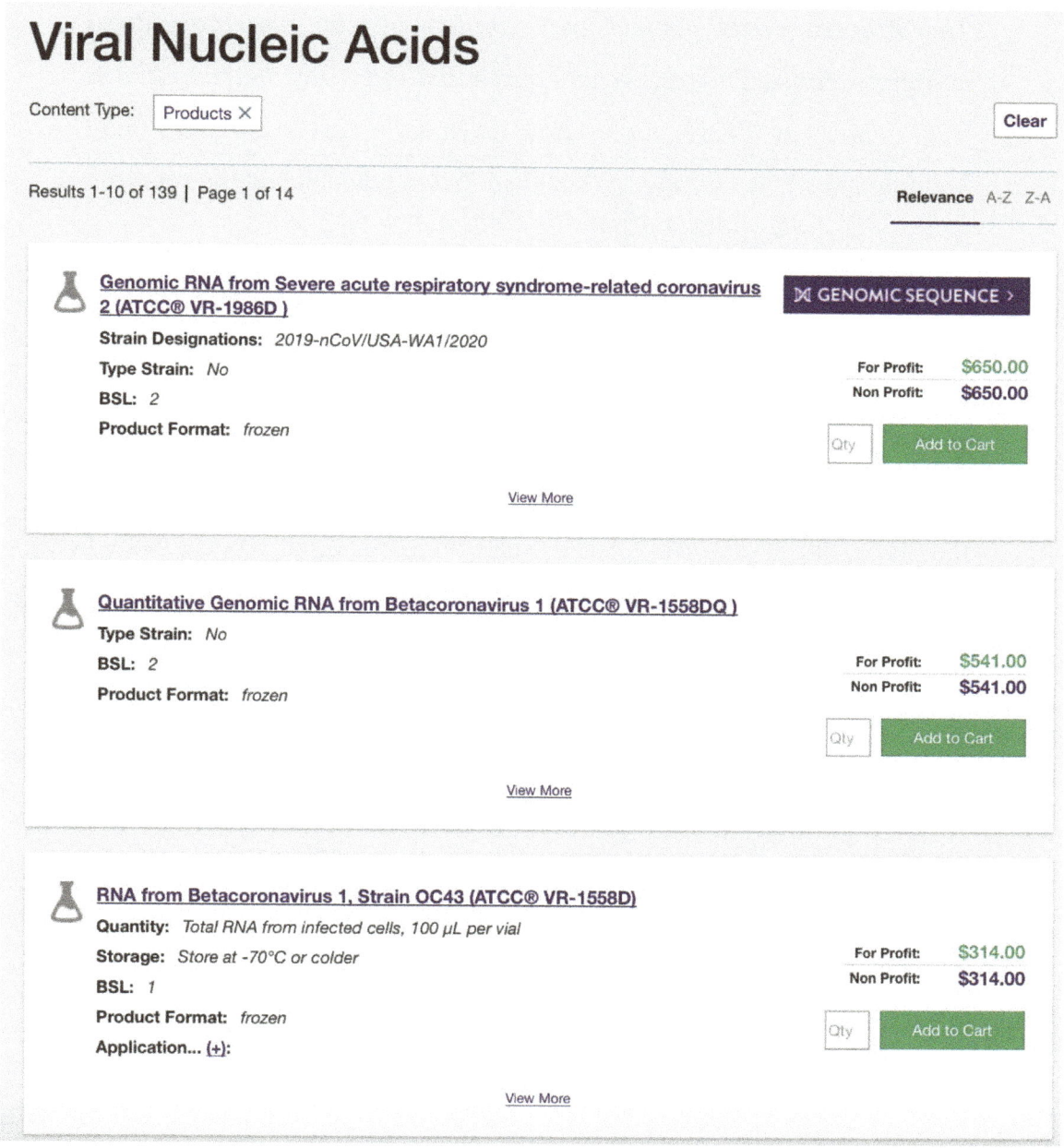

Genomic RNA Building Blocks For Sale That Comprise Coronaviruses (2020)

Smallpox is yet another case in point. Scientists at the University of Alberta, Canada, have engineered the virus scHPXV, which causes Horsepox, a virus so closely related to the Variola virus that making one means you can make the other, something like this: if you can manufacture a Tesla Model X, then you can surely manufacture a Tesla Model S.[35]

---

[35] It is illegal to create the virus responsible for Smallpox in a commercial laboratory.

The Alberta virus project was funded by the pharmaceutical company Tonix. *The researchers purchased their DNA building blocks from publicly available sources. How much did it cost to purchase these building blocks? According to Dr. David Evans, who headed the research team, a mere $100,000 dollars.*

Tonix Pharmaceutical eventually produced a vaccine from their genomic project. Why didn't the Alberta team simply get their Horsepox virus from readily available sources in nature?

In order for Tonix Pharmaceutical to be able to patent their vaccine, they had to create it from scratch in their lab.

Smallpox, like SARS-CoV-2, is a droplet infection. Smallpox is deadly because of how the Variola virus causes its victim to bleed out from the inside. At least 30 percent of people who contract smallpox will progress to septic shock and die. This virus has killed over a half *billion* people in the 20th century alone. The Smallpox virus had been around since at least as far back as during the height of the Egyptian empire.

Smallpox was eradicated from the earth in 1980 because of one thing and one thing only: the Smallpox vaccine.

Samples of the virus only exist in isolation for research under lock and key at undisclosed location(s).

The history of the development of the Smallpox vaccine by British physician Dr. Edward Jenner in 1796 is a good introduction to some of the work conducted in today's virology labs. Dr. Jenner has saved more lives than any other person who ever lived or is living, because of his great observational discernment and strong constitution required to confront the bloodletters, shamans, and snake-oil salesmen who made their living treating Smallpox victims and did not welcome a cure. Dr. Jenner observed that milkmaids who had been exposed to Cowpox showed immunity to the Smallpox virus.

"In 1796, Jenner was approached by Sarah Nelmes, a dairymaid, who had caught cowpox from a cow named Blossom. Jenner scratched pus from the blister on her hand onto the arm of James Phipps, an eight-

year-old boy who had never contracted cowpox or smallpox," Gower said. "Phipps became slightly ill with cowpox, but soon made a full recovery. Jenner then attempted to variolate Phipps, to expose him to smallpox, in order to test whether or not he was now immune. As Jenner had expected, and to everyone's relief, Phipps did not contract smallpox. Over the next two years, Jenner carried out the experiment on different subjects before writing up and publishing his work. Jenner named the new technique 'vaccine inoculation', later shortened to 'vaccination,' after the Latin 'vacca' for cow." [36]

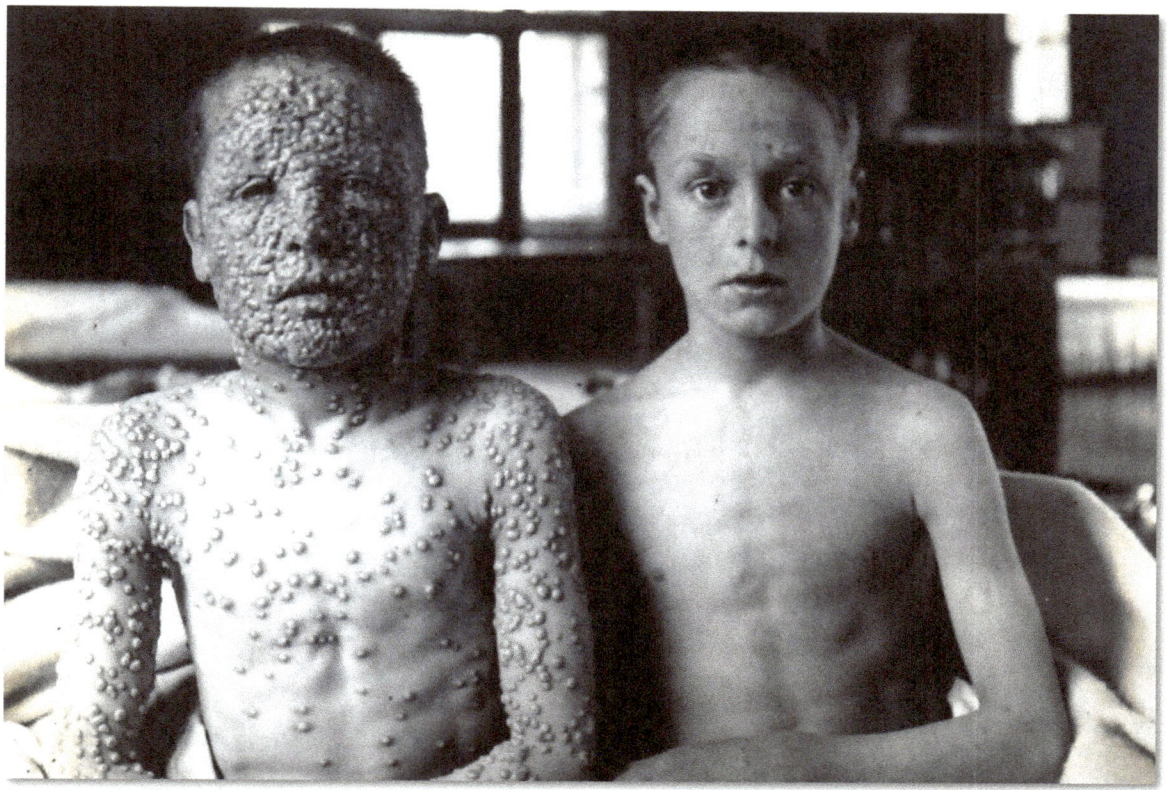

This iconic photo of two boys – one vaccinated against smallpox and one who hadn't been vaccinated – was published in 1901, and taken by Dr. Allan Warner at the Leicester Isolation Hospital. Photo / The Jenner Trust [37]

Genetically engineering and/or modifying an existent pathogen in order to make it more virulent certainly can be motivated by malevolent intent, as would be in the case in germ warfare, but more often in today's world such research is driven

---

[36] New Zealand Herald. *Smallpox and the photos anti-vaxxers don't want you to see.* By: L.J. Charleston, June 9, 2019.
[37] Ibid.

by pecuniary motivations that center around providing a treatment for some of mankind's most pernicious diseases while being able to patent their creation.

Dr. Ralph Baric of the University of North Carolina took a dangerous SARS virus responsible for the pandemic of 2002-2004 [38] and purposefully made it more virulent by replacing proteins to the naturally occurring SARS. The result?

The genetically modified SARS 2.0 created in Dr. Baric's lab was immune to vaccines and resistant to treatments that worked for the original SARS.

Dr. Baric explained why his lab created this more virulent strain of SARS: Because it could mutate and become resistant to our existing vaccines. The idea is that by creating a deadlier mutated virus, we could develop stronger vaccines that will save us from a more lethal SARS epidemic—that is, if the natural SARS ever mutates.[39] The current author would modify Dr. Baric's observation in one way: "The question is not *if* SARS will mutate, but *when* and *how* it will mutate."

Forensic Issues: SARS-CoV-2

I remind the reader that all classes of viruses originated in nature[40] but that their discrete variations when compared to their original blueprint could be the product of intelligent design, mutation, or a combination thereof with **naturally occurring mutations as the most prevalent means by which a virus' genome is modified.**

We can begin to investigate the forensic mystery of where SARS-CoV-2 originated by examining what it is about it that makes it different from its closest relative. Sometimes this forensic puzzle is similar to distinguishing between natural and manmade geological formations. Lay people can tell the difference between, for

---

[38] The virus outbreak of 2002 began in Guangdong province located in southeastern China. The disease that resulted would become known as SARS, or severe acute respiratory syndrome. It took only a few months for 8,096 people in 26 countries to become infected with the new viral illness, which eventually led to 774 deaths.

[39] Nature (2015, November) by Declan Butler. *Engineered bat virus stirs debate over risky research. Lab-made coronavirus related to SARS can infect human cells*

[40] Please refer to The International Committee on Taxonomy of Viruses.

example, the Eiffel Tower and a sand dune in Sub Saharan Africa. But when the question becomes distinguishing between a home designed by Frank Lloyd Wright or Daniel Lieberman, or SARS-CoV-1 and SARS CoV-2, the puzzle is not so easy to solve if all you have to go on are the epidemiological manifestations of the disease caused by the virus(es).

I gently remind the reader, especially those who love to read mystery novels, that responsible public health behavior is unrelated to and distinct from the etiology of any one particular pathogen. Intelligence agencies and their governments may be very much interested in the origins of troubling viruses like SARS-CoV-2 for any number of legitimate reasons; but the general public's primary role in any pandemic is to behave in a socially responsible way; that is, pathogen-aversive based upon the science of contagion dynamics. What follows are some forensic observations and analyses of SARS-CoV-2's presentation.

The Chinese government, especially its public health ministries, appeared to be caught off guard when doctors in the vicinity of Wuhan began seeing patients with severe respiratory distress that did not respond to conventional treatments. Napoleon Legal Consulting, Inc., performed its proprietary Forensic Profiling and Human Factor Analysis Analysis[41] on the writings and spoken proclamations from various Chinese agencies and doctors who were first to recognize a peculiarly virulent form of what was labeled at the time "pneumonia." In January of 2020, *The Lancet* published the following, which associated the infamous Huanan seafood market with the cases but did not conclude that the market was the proximate source of the infections that local doctors in Wuhan were seeing in their emergency rooms, to wit:

"By Jan 2, 2020, 41 admitted hospital patients had been identified as having laboratory-confirmed 2019-nCoV infection. Most of the infected patients were men (30 [73%] of 41); less than half had underlying

---

[41] Forensic Profile Analysis (FPA) and Human Factor Analysis (HFA) are proprietary to Napoleon Legal Consulting, Inc. They are investigative tools/methods that are designed to reveal embedded meaning within various human productions. Productions include crime scenes, witness behavior, and visual image data (in-person still photos and video), as well as behavioral patterns in various social, familial and vocational contexts. Productions include written and spoken expressions.

diseases (13 [32%]), including diabetes (eight [20%]), hypertension (six [15%]), and cardiovascular disease (six [15%]). Median age was 49·0 years (IQR 41·0–58·0). 27 (66%) of 41 patients had been exposed to Huanan seafood market. One family cluster was found. Common symptoms at onset of illness were fever (40 [98%] of 41 patients), cough (31 [76%]), and myalgia or fatigue (18 [44%]); less common symptoms were sputum production (11 [28%] of 39), headache (three [8%] of 38), haemoptysis (two [5%] of 39), and diarrhoea (one [3%] of 38). Dyspnoea developed in 22 (55%) of 40 patients (median time from illness onset to dyspnoea 8·0 days [IQR 5·0–13·0]). 26 (63%) of 41 patients had lymphopenia. All 41 patients had pneumonia with abnormal findings on chest CT. Complications included acute respiratory distress syndrome (12 [29%]), RNAaemia (six [15%]), acute cardiac injury (five [12%]) and secondary infection (four [10%]). 13 (32%) patients were admitted to an ICU and six (15%) died. Compared with non-ICU patients, ICU patients had higher plasma levels of IL2, IL7, IL10, GSCF, IP10, MCP1, MIP1A, and TNFα. Interpretation The 2019-nCoV infection caused clusters of severe respiratory illness similar to severe acute respiratory syndrome coronavirus and was associated with ICU admission and high mortality. Major gaps in our knowledge of the origin, epidemiology, duration of human transmission, and clinical spectrum of disease need fulfillment by future studies." [42]

One of the more interesting things about this study is that it found the "Symptom onset of the first patient was on December 1, 2019 and had NO relation to the Huanan Seafood Market." (Emphasis added) Moreover, the researchers found that "No epidemiological link was found between the first patient and later cases." This suggests that SARS-CoV-2 had already made its way into the community and was at work spreading itself. Of the 41 patients studied, 14 had no *obvious* connection to

---

[42] The Lancet: Clinical features of patients infected with 2019 novel Corona virus in Wuhan, China. Volume 395, Issue 10223, P497-506, February 15, 2020.

the infamous wet market.[43] The word "obvious" doesn't mean that there is not a more shrouded link to the market; it merely means nothing immediately jumped out at the researchers looking into this issue at the time.

While some people find the 14-patient "no obvious connection" sample suspicious, the fact that 27 of those infected *were* immediately traced back to exposure to the Huanan market is a nominal finding IF SARS-CoV-2 had already entered the community, either from that market or cross-pollinating from an infection spread sequence that was already in progress.

Some have made note of the fact that bats, living or dead, were not sold at the Huanan market, an observation that is **totally irrelevant** given that an intermediate species **other than a bat** is a usual and customary link in the infection chain leading to human infection, if the virus was of a natural origin. It is the intermediate animal sold at these wet markets that would be of interest, not the immune carrier of this particular virus; that is, the bat. Getting back to the absence of bats sold at the Huanan market, and once again that assertion is unproven, but regardless, any number of other living species, including those identified by National Geographic's investigative journalists found *routinely* for sale all over China, including the Huanan market, could have *easily* served the role of intermediate host between bats and people, to wit:

> *"The Huanan market, for example, had a wild animal section where live and slaughtered species were for sale including snakes, beavers, pangolins, porcupines, and baby crocodiles, among other animals."*[44]

To further buttress our assertions, let me share with you a study published in the journal *Current Biology* that compared the genomic structure of the *pangolin* SARS-CoV-2 virus to the human SARS-CoV-2 virus, to wit:

---

[43] The descriptor "wet" derives from the blood, saliva, urine and feces, and other liquids part and parcel to animal slaughter. As we will make the case later in this book, all animal slaughter by its very nature is wet; therefore, virus amplification as a threat should not be limited to stereotypical "wet" markets. The only reason American consumers don't recognize the "wet" nature of their meat market is because the "wet" part is out of sight, therefore, out of mind.

[44] National Geographic: 'Wet markets' likely launched the coronavirus. Here's what you need to know. By: Dina Fine Maron, February 15, 2020.

Highlights
- Pangolin-CoV is 91.02% identical to SARS-CoV-2 at the whole-genome level
- Pangolin-CoV is the second closest relative of SARS-CoV-2 behind RaTG13
- Five key amino acids in the RBD are consistent between Pangolin-CoV and SARS-CoV-2
- Only SARS-CoV-2 contains a potential cleavage site for furin proteases

Pangolin soon to be butchered alive to the first buyer

The authors went on to say this: *"Conclusively, this study suggests that pangolin species are a natural reservoir of SARS-CoV-2-like CoVs."* [45]

I will remind the reader once again that given the subtleties of virus replication and spread, not to mention the cross-pollination that occurs between naturally occurring viral mutations and human's efforts to modify them, the source of the virus responsible for the COVID-19 pandemic would likely be unprovable in a criminal court of law. I will also add that as I write this sentence, SARS-CoV-2 may very well be mutating in discrete ways, perhaps involving the spike (S) protein structures that allow the virus to unlock its host's cells. This means that tracking down a source(s) may be practically impossible. This is simply the way viruses have always worked since time immemorial. Given incubation time tables for this novel

---

[45] Current Biology (2020) Tao Zhang, Qunfu Wu, Zhigang Zhang. Probable Pangolin Origin of SARS-CoV-2 Associated with the COVID-19 Outbreak. Volume 30, Issue 8, 20 April 2020, Pages 1578.

virus, it would not be surprising to find that SARS-CoV-2 had already entered the community as early as November of 2019, if not sooner.

I now want to share a forensic mindset, were we to indulge those people who believe (not know) that a virology lab created SARS-CoV-2. If the puzzle is to identify the lab responsible for SARS-CoV-2, if in fact the virus was intelligently designed, then the reader should realize the complexity of the task at hand. Labs all over the world have been examining how CoVs infect their hosts for more than 50 years. These labs have also been tinkering with these viruses' structures and genome for that long, if not longer. This makes sense because experts in virology have known for a very, very long time that a likely candidate responsible for the next pandemic will be one of the SARS classes of viruses.

Virology labs exist in every state within the USA capable of modifying SARS viruses. [46] Funding for these virology labs has come from private, public, and so-called "dark" sources.

> "In 2014, the National Institutes of Health (NIH) approved a grant to *EcoHealth Alliance* designated for research into "Understanding the Risk of Bat Corona virus Emergence." The project involved collaborating with researchers at the Wuhan Institute of Virology in China to study Coronaviruses in bats and the risk of potential transfer to humans. The original five-year grant was reapproved by the Trump administration in July 2019. In total, $3,378,896 in NIH funding was directed from the government to the project. The project, which was established "to understand what factors allow Coronaviruses, including close relatives to SARS, to evolve and jump into the human population," yielded 20 scientific reports on how zoonotic diseases may transfer from bats to humans."
> [47] In the latter part of April 2020 President Trump discontinued this particular NIH Coronavirus funding.

---

[46] http://www.virology.net/garryfavwebvirlabs.html
[47] USA Today. Fact check: Obama administration did not send $3.7 million to Wuhan lab. By: Matthew Brown and Kim Hjelmgaard, May 4, 2020.

Still, when we find an especially sophisticated virology laboratory right in the middle of where COVID-19 patient zero, or low number, lived, we should not ignore that fact and do further investigation.

Wuhan Institute of Virology

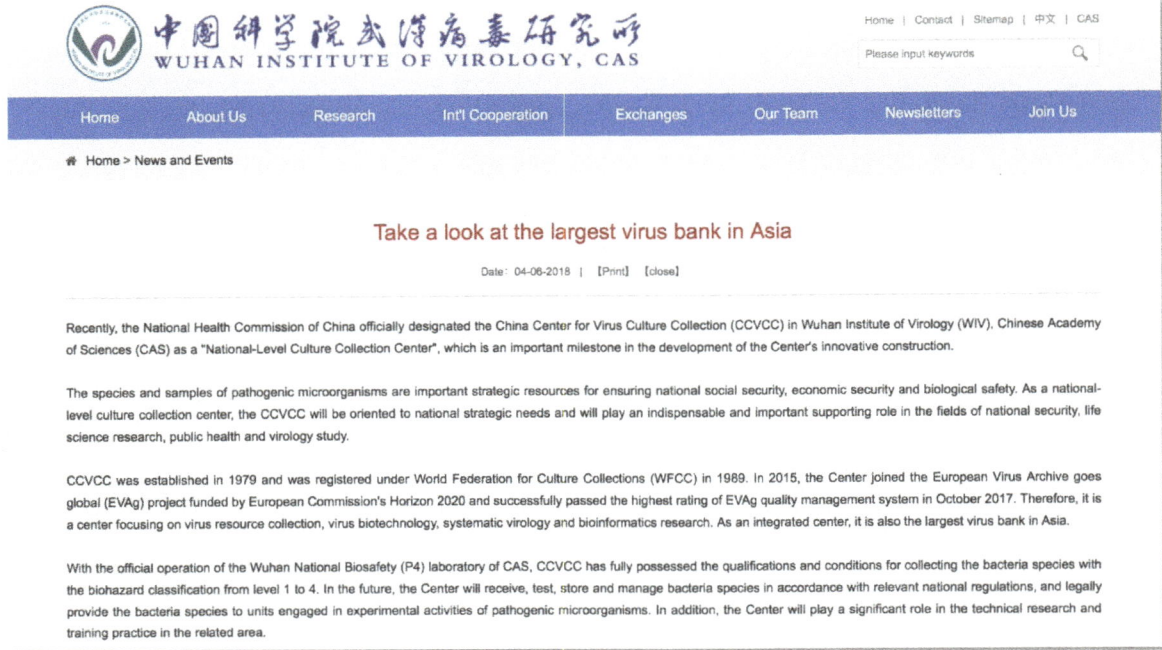

One of the things that jumps out from this press release is the fact that The Wuhan Institute of Virology (WIV) contains the largest virus bank in the world, underscore *world*. Note that the WIV makes no effort to hide the fact that its bank is replete with pathogenic viruses that are "important *strategic* resources for ensuring national social security." In military-speak, those words are the sine qua non of "germ warfare." "Life science research and public health" were cordoned off descriptors of "why" the world's largest virus bank exists, which supports our assertion.

We know WIV has the world's largest store of pathogenic viruses.[48] We also know that China's researchers have been monitoring various outbreaks of very troubling and dangerous viruses secondary to the meat industry for years, like

---

[48] *One of the world's* largest stores of pathogenic viruses is more likely, given the successful efforts on behalf of other countries to shroud their work in this area.

virtually every other lab in the world. Those outbreaks and specific viruses responsible for these meat-farming outbreaks can be found under a heading within this book entitled: (*How to Play Russian Roulette with Viruses*)

Richard H. Ebright, PhD, who is an American molecular biologist and widely recognized expert on CoVs, stated:

> *"Wuhan CDC and Wuhan Institute of Virology conducted large research projects on novel bat viruses, maintained large research collections of novel bat viruses, and possessed the virus that is the most closely related known virus in the world to the outbreak virus. Documentary evidence indicates that the novel-bat-virus projects at Wuhan CDC and Wuhan Institute of Virology used PPE and bio-safety standards that would pose high risk of accidental infection of a laboratory worker upon contact with a virus having the transmission properties of the outbreak virus. Laboratory accidents and especially laboratory acquired infections are common."* [49]

A key point that needs to be stressed is one that is obvious, but only once it is articulated. SARS-CoV-2 had entered the community in late 2019 to the tune of billions upon billions of viruses. The viruses' victims were obviously fewer in number. SARS-CoV-2 stricken patients were showing up at local hospitals during this time, and some hospitals took mucous membrane swab samples (similar to how people are tested today) and sent them to any number of labs, some of which were gene sequencing labs, in order to identify the pathogen causing this refractory illness. Health officials in China put an end to this uncoordinated effort on the part of hospitals to identify this pathogen and ordered the samples in "unauthorized" labs to all be destroyed, which is exactly what should have been done in order to limit the number of vectors, human and non-human, of this rogue virus. We now have formal documentation of this, to wit:

> *Liu Dengfeng, an official with the National Health Commission's science and education department, said this was done at unauthorized*

---
[49] Sunday Guardian Live: Corona leaked likely from Wuhan Institute of Virology: Experts. By: Abhinandan Mishra & Dibyendu Mondal, April 25, 2020.

labs to "prevent the risk to laboratory biological safety and prevent secondary disasters caused by unidentified pathogens". [50]

On February 29, 2020, Chinese magazine Caixin, certainly not a Communist party mouthpiece, published an article—at great risk to the investigative journalists involved—that included its exhaustive investigation of what happened during the early stages of what we now label the COVID-19 outbreak before anyone knew any details about the pathogen, including the name of the virus that we now label SARS-CoV-2. Here are the pertinent details discovered by Caixin's investigative reporters:

- *"As early as Dec. 27, a Guangzhou-based genomics company had sequenced most of the virus from fluid samples from the lung of a 65-year old deliveryman who worked at the seafood market where many of the first cases emerged. The results showed an alarming similarity to the deadly SARS coronavirus that killed nearly 800 people between 2002 and 2003.*
- *Around that time, local doctors sent at least eight other patient samples from hospitals around Wuhan to multiple Chinese genomics companies, including industry heavyweight BGI, as they worked to determine what was behind a growing number of cases of unexplained respiratory disease. The results all pointed to a dangerous SARS-like virus.*
- *China notified the World Health Organization (WHO) on Dec. 31, 2019 about the emergence of an unidentified infectious disease, two weeks before it shared the virus's genome sequence with the world, and crucially, more than three weeks before Chinese authorities confirmed publicly that the virus was spreading between people.*

At this point, I would interject a reminder to all amateur sleuths that as of December 31, 2019, China had handed the baton to the World Health Organization. WHO had more than enough data regarding the seriousness of

---

[50] South China Morning Post. China confirms unauthorized labs were told to destroy early coronavirus samples. Story by: Zhuang Pinghui in Beijing.

this novel pathogen and arguably the obligation to put the entire world on notice before the end of 2019.

- *Concerns about the new disease were initially kept within a small group of medical workers, researchers and officials. On Dec. 30, Dr. Li Wenliang was one of several in Wuhan who sounded the first alarms and released initial evidence online. Li, who was punished for releasing the information, would perish from the disease five weeks later, after contracting it from a patient.*

- *On Jan. 1, after several batches of genome sequence results had been returned to hospitals and submitted to health authorities, an employee of one genomics company received a phone call from an official at the Hubei Provincial Health Commission, ordering the company to stop testing samples from Wuhan related to the new disease and destroy all existing samples. The employee spoke on condition of anonymity, saying they were told to immediately cease releasing test results and information about the tests, and report any future results to authorities.*

- *Then on Jan. 3, China's National Health Commission (NHC), the nation's top health authority, ordered institutions not to publish any information related to the unknown disease, and ordered labs to transfer any samples they had to designated testing institutions, or to destroy them. The order, which Caixin has seen, did not specify any designated testing institutions.*

- *It was Jan. 9 when Chinese authorities finally announced that a novel coronavirus was behind Wuhan's viral pneumonia outbreak. Even then, the transmissibility of the virus was downplayed, leaving the public unaware of the imminent danger.*

- *Finally, on Jan. 20, Zhong Nanshan, a leading authority on respiratory health who came to national attention in his role*

> *fighting SARS, confirmed in a TV interview that the disease was spreading from person-to-person.[51]*

According to Caixin's and others' investigations, little doubt exists that Chinese officials made no concerted effort to communicate outside of the WHO about its developing data set regarding the severity of COVID-19 and its genomic structure, which I believe was known to them as early as December 31, 2019. Forcing doctors and labs to go dark with their knowledge early on may have been motivated by Chinese officials' belief that they could internally manage this rogue virus before news of its severity got out. Don't forget, WHO had been made fully aware of the data regarding this novel pathogen's virulence and potential for widespread infection before the end of 2019. Given Chinese officials' experience with previous virus pandemics and their economic impact upon China's economy, their decision was grossly negligent but does come with a degree of plausible deniability, given that the WHO's official role was to inform the world of what they knew and China had provided more than enough data for them to sound the alarm. Nevertheless, by enforcing a blackout of information, China was gambling not only with their money, but the world's money. China lost the bet and so did everyone else in the casino. The more serious accusation made by the Trump administration's Trade and Manufacturing Policy Director Peter Navarro alleges that China's forced blackout was part of Chinese officials' plan to "seed" the world with the SARS-CoV-2 virus. That accusation, if proven true, could fall under any number of international law provisions that conceivably could result in a prosecution of the principals involved, including the General Secretary of the Communist Party of China, Xi Jinping. To wit:

> *"Under Article 1 of the International Law Commission's 2001 Responsibility of States for Internationally Wrongful Acts, states are responsible for their internationally wrongful acts. Under Article 2,*

---

[51] CAIXIN: February 29, 2020. *In Depth: How Early Signs of a SARS-Like Virus Were Spotted, Spread, and Throttled.* By: Gao Yu, Peng Yanfeng, Yang Rui, Feng Yuding, Ma Danmeng, Flynn Murphy, Han Wei and Timmy Shen.

"Wrongful acts" are those that are "attributable to the state" and that "constitute a breach of an international obligation." Under Article 4, Conduct is attributable to the state when it is an act of state through the executive, legislative, or judicial functions of the central government. These abrogations of international law could reach all the all the way up to Xi Jinping, the general secretary of the Chinese Communist Party."[52]

Dr. Shi Zhengli

The reader may have been persuaded to believe that Dr. Shi Zhengli is the Steve Jobs of CoVs. And while Dr. Shi Zhengli is certainly at the top of her field, she is by no means the only virologist who had or has the ability to decipher the genomic fingerprint for any of the SARS-CoVs and the ability to modify their genomes. Her research is logically and without surprise focused upon how an infection with CoVs can spill over[53] from bats, in particular the horseshoe bat, to infect humans, and the biology of exactly how these and other viruses break into their host's cells.[54] Dr. Shi Zhengli has worked for years with bat CoVs at her lab at WIV. It was she and her team at WIV that discovered the natural bat reservoir for the SARS pathogen that spread in southern China from 2002 to 2003.

---

[52] International Law Commission Report, A/56/10 August 2001. See: https://legal.un.org/ilc/
[53] Spillover infection, also known as pathogen spillover and spillover event, occurs when a reservoir population with high pathogen prevalence comes into contact with a novel host population. The pathogen is transmitted from the reservoir population and may or may not be transmitted within the host population.
[54] The SARS-CoV-2 virus is most closely related to Coronaviruses, which can be found in certain populations of horseshoe bats that live in Yunnan province, China, located approximately 1,000 miles (1,600 kilometers) from Wuhan, China.

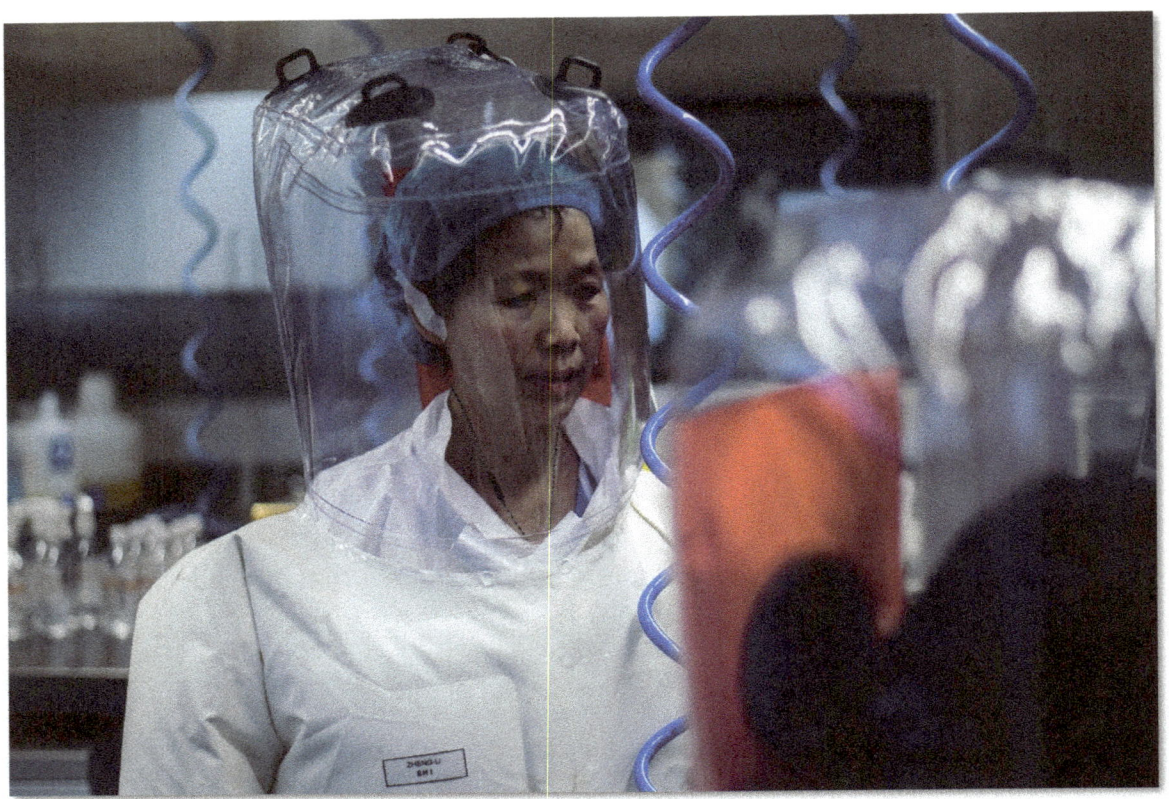

Dr. Shi Zhengli at her Lab at the WIV

In February, Dr. Zhengli communicated through *We Chat* to deny that SARS-CoV-2 originated in her lab. She stated quite confidently, "I guarantee it with my life." Our FPA analysis found Dr. Zhengli's proclamations to be genuine, that is, she believed her own assertion. She also made the following statement, which our analysis found to be a direct reference to China's notorious wet markets and the world's meat industry:

> "The 2019 novel Coronavirus is a punishment by nature to human's unsanitary lifestyles." [55]

Lots of things about Dr. Zhengli's spontaneous proclamations suggest that she did not have a direct hand in creating SARS-CoV-2 in its complete form. Moreover, I believe she never served in the witting role of agent for the alleged Chinese Government's COVID-19 weapons project that included a

---

[55] In Mandarin Chinese, the word "unsanitary" not only means dirty but also means unhealthy lifestyles, as in choice of diet and therefore likely to cause disease. 不卫生的；不干净的

complete genome of SARS-CoV-2. [56] And as a point of order, no legal proof exists that would support the existence of such a program. Her statements suggest the complete opposite. Going back at least ten or more years, Dr. Zhengli has **vociferously** sounded the alarm about how SARS viruses, aka CoVs, are likely to be the culprit in the next great pandemic. Her warnings centered on human behavior, with a particular emphasis upon unsanitary *lifestyles* as found in wet markets—and by logical extension, the meat industry. Such proclamations continually made in three different languages to media outlets all over the world is NOT the behavior of a virologist engaged in clandestine projects that plan to create, then release, a deadly virus that may as well have her name on it, given how people tend to ascribe guilt by association and genomic tracking technology. Our FPA analysis also found Dr. Zhengli's spontaneous reaction to her first recognition of the SARS-CoV-2 outbreak to be TOTALLY INCONSISTENT with mal- or misfeasance on her part, to wit:

> *"I had never expected this kind of thing to happen in Wuhan, in central China."* Her studies had shown that the southern, subtropical provinces of Guangdong, Guangxi and Yunnan have the greatest risk of Coronaviruses jumping to humans from animals—particularly bats, a known reservoir. If Coronaviruses were the culprit, she remembers thinking, "Could they have come from our lab?"[57]

Forensically speaking, Dr. Zhengli's spontaneously uttered rhetorical question, *"Could they have come from our lab?"* would be no different from a situation where a wife, upon learning that her husband had been poisoned to death, commented to the police: "I hope I didn't poison him." Dr. Zhengli also made an exhaustive inventory of all the genomic samples from her lab that had been disposed of and compared them to the critically important nucleotides in SARS-CoV-2—they did not match. 'That really took a load off my mind. I had not slept a wink for days."

---

[56] Of all the "germs" that can be used in germ warfare, SARS viruses, and in particular SARS-CoV-2, are relatively poor choices to weaponize for reasons well beyond the scope of this book.
[57] Scientific American. How China's 'Bat Woman' Hunted Down Viruses from SARS to the New Corona virus. By: Jane Qiu on April 27, 2020.

Spontaneous utterances, as they are referred to in American jurisprudence, are given great weight, because such utterances are made before reflection and self-interest can be factored into a statement on what might be or become a problematic subject. The same principle is applied to deathbed utterances. In order to legally link SARS-CoV-2 to WIV beyond a reasonable doubt, one would have to have a bulletproof genomic sequence paper trail, complete with time stamps, that identically matched the first SARS-CoV-19 genomic sequence taken from its first victim.

We have reason to believe that other well-known genomic sequencing labs had gotten their hands on complete SARS-CoV-2 viruses even before they had a name.

- December 24-27, 2019—**Vision Medicals**, a genomics company based in Huangpu district in Guangzhou, South China's Guangdong province, were provided lung source samples from a patient in Wuhan, China. **Vision Medicals** shared their genomic sequencing findings with **Chinese Academy of Medical Sciences**.
- December 27, 2019—The Central Hospital of Wuhan sent swabs from a second patient with the mysterious pneumonia to Beijing-based lab **CapitalBio Medlab Co. Ltd.** for study.
- December 26-30, 2019—The Central Hospital of Wuhan sent another genomic lab, **BGI**, at least 30 samples from different pneumonia cases for sequencing. Three were found to contain the new Coronavirus. In addition to the Dec. 26 case, the second and third positive samples were received on Dec. 29 and Dec. 30. They were tested together and ***the results were reported to the Wuhan Municipal Health Commission as early as Jan. 1, 2020.***
- January 1, 2020—Gene sequencing companies received an order from Hubei's health commission to stop testing and destroy all samples, according to an employee at one. "If you test it in the future, be sure to report it to us," the person said they were told by phone.

- Jan. 3, 2020—the **National Health Commission** issued its gag order and said the Wuhan pneumonia samples needed to be treated as highly pathogenic microorganisms — and that any samples needed to be moved to approved testing facilities, or destroyed.
- January 10, 2020—Chinese scientists published the complete genome of SARS-CoV-2 and provided it to **GenBank.**
- February 14, 2020—Complete versions of the SARS-CoV-2 were delivered to the **University of Maryland** from the CDC. [58]

What the current author finds fascinating, but not necessarily surprising, is that investigators at Caixin spoke with a virologist who stated, *"Even the Wuhan Institute of Virology (WIV) under the Chinese Academy of Sciences was not qualified for the tests and told to destroy samples in its lab."* From a forensic scientist's prism, excluding WIV as a preferred lab suggests some intriguing reasonable possibilities. One possibility is that Chinese officials felt Dr. Shi Zhengli could not be trusted to keep the novel virus' genomic sequence secret—a fear well founded in that Dr. Zhengli has been a prolific publisher of her lab's discoveries over her entire career. If Chinese health officials wanted to keep this burgeoning pandemic under wraps, Dr. Zhengli would be a poor choice to conscript into their plans. Given what we know about the SARS-CoV-2 trail, a trail that was first picked up before this rogue virus had a name; human behavior intervened and made a bad problem worse. Denial, deceit, fear, hubris—as in perhaps "we can manage this without the world finding out" —and the ever-present bureaucratic Kitty Genovese[59] defect are right at the top of the list of human behavior dynamics that brought us to this point.

---

[58] CAIXIN: February 29, 2020. *In Depth: How Early Signs of a SARS-Like Virus Were Spotted, Spread, and Throttled.* By: Gao Yu, Peng Yanfeng, Yang Rui, Feng Yuding, Ma Danmeng, Flynn Murphy, Han Wei and Timmy Shen.

[59] The Kitty Genovese Effect: In the early hours of March 13, 1964, 28-year-old Kitty Genovese was stabbed outside the apartment building across the street from where she lived, in an apartment above a row of shops on Austin Street, in the Kew Gardens neighborhood of Queens in New York City. Two weeks after the murder, The New York Times published an article claiming that 38 witnesses saw or heard the attack, but none of them called the police or came to her aid. The psychological dynamic that resulted in no one taking action was because witnesses to the murder assumed someone else would call the police.

Human beings have been intelligently tinkering with virulent viruses for a very long time. The inter-relationship between individual labs and GenBank serving as a shared central hub is a public health-positive arrangement. For those who think identifying the "bad guy" when it comes to SARS-CoV-2 is no different than identifying a 7/11 robber on a surveillance cam, you are sorely mistaken. Unlike human criminals, in the virus world, killers often act alone.

Politics, The Media Entertainment Complex and The General Public

Human behavior is inextricably linked to the COVID-19 black swan event. Once we found ourselves in the middle of the latest of a long history of pandemics, we couldn't get out of our own way because of our customs, fears, and self-destructive tendency to game everything we come in contact with, along with the seemingly insatiable need for everyone from politicians to social media stars to exploit every national tragedy so they can be a "somebody."

Politicians schooled in political science and the law had no idea what was happening with these invisible terrors that had been given names more confusing to them than the names given to artificial sweeteners. And if they didn't know what and why it was happening, they surely had no idea as to what to do. So they did the only thing they know how: they imposed blunt force behavioral modification edicts on citizens who already didn't trust them before anyone had ever heard of COVID-19.

Even when the edicts were correct, a public jaded by partisan maneuvering on the part of some of our most influential national institutions wasn't reassured. In fact many people felt worse, more confused, and even more distrustful. Social media types who saw their chance to game this latest national tragedy didn't help matters by encouraging oppositional behaviors in response to common-sense public health recommendations because of their own obstreperous personality typology, and because they saw their chance to gain more followers or friends, all in the name of freedom from tyranny. And as with all social media, because a microphone came with signing up for Twitter, Facebook, Instagram, Tik-Tok, et al, does not mean, therefore, that the microphone came with an advanced degree on contagion dynamics—or for that matter, common sense.

As if social media behavior related to COVID-19 is not enough proof of the disastrous consequences of providing free microphones to anyone with a social media account, a recently settled work-related disability lawsuit filed by Facebook moderators (those people who are forced to watch the content produced by the general public) should leave no doubt in your mind. Facebook moderators were paid $52 million as part of a settlement after all of them developed any number of disabling mental health issues, including PTSD, after having to watch snuff videos of people and animals being viciously tortured, which included their consumption while alive (a not uncommon practice all over the world), along with perverted sexual abuse of puppies, kittens, and infants. [60]

Unless we as a species get a grip on our own self-assured venality, and if we don't find the courage to replace our human foibles with a more sophisticated understanding of the fact that we are more often than not the designers of our own bad fortune, and most certainly the fortunes of every other species we come into contact with, then in the future there won't be black swan events for you to have to deal with, because by then we will have killed off all the black swans.

The media entertainment complex, which long ago retreated from the ideal of objective reportage, uses every presentation sleight of hand in the book to take any fact, opinion, declaration, or non-verbal mannerism related to COVID-19 from a political adversary or anyone else their owners disagree with and use it against them, going so far as to ruin their adversaries' professional and personal lives. You can also count on the fact that when one of their kindred spirits commits an unconscionable act, e.g., one that made SARS-CoV-2 spread with greater efficiency, that bad actor can count on their friends in the media entertainment complex to run

---

[60] Dow Jones Marketwatch (May 12, 2020) Facebook to pay $52 million in settlement with content moderators who developed PTSD.

interference for them—as is most often the case, as they say in journalism, "bury the lead."

Here is but one example. The media entertainment complex collectively failed to put a spotlight on Speaker of the House Nancy Pelosi (D) CA., who staged a video-op, in of all places Chinatown, in order to fuel animus against the President who shuttered travel from China early on in COVID-19's course against the wishes of at least one of his senior infectious disease medical advisors. In a venal display of partisan, opportunistic political theater, where she accused President Trump of racism, Speaker Pelosi encouraged the residents of Chinatown to stand right in the middle of the railroad tracks for the SARS-CoV-2 express from Wuhan, China, as it came barreling down on them.

KRON Channel 4 San Francisco February 24, 2020

We know as fact Speaker Pelosi was in possession of intelligence which motivated, at least in part, President Trump's decision to shutter travel from China. I paraphrase: "Tens of thousands of residents who reside in hot spots of COVID-19 virus got wind of the impending lockdown soon to be imposed by the Chinese government. As a result, high-risk residents with higher incomes will flood our country if steps are not taken soon to prevent their entry into the U.S."

We also know that Speaker Pelosi, as third in line to become President should anything happen to President Trump or Vice President Pence, had immediate and unfettered access to experts in virology and infectious diseases who were all, to the person, referring to SARS-CoV-2 as a defcon-1 event BEFORE February 24, 2020, when Speaker Pelosi staged this theatrical event. Speaker Pelosi knew or should have known at the time she staged her political theater in Chinatown that SARS-CoV-2 was highly contagious, that social distancing mandates would be implemented soon, and that people would be required to wear facemasks—yet, her political theater stage play was more important to her than the health and safety of the residents of Chinatown.

A serious, potentially deadly problem manifests when politicians who majored in political theater are put in charge of a deadly pandemic. People, in this case, the Speaker of the House, third in succession to become President, know nothing about basic biological science and in particular viruses, but what she does know a lot about is how to choreograph political gamesmanship. She is very good at that—and to be candid, so is President Trump.

Rather than the press call out Speaker of the House Pelosi for organizing a gathering in Chinatown in response to President Trump's shuttering of travel from China, the media entertainment complex sat on the story like a mother hen protecting her chicks from the rain. No wonder we can't get the average person to adopt responsible public health guidelines when they know that virtually everything they see and hear is political theater, and the reviewers of these poorly acted stage plays are in bed with their favored writers, directors and actors.

What passes for reporter's questions these days, and we saw and continue to see ample evidence of this during the COVID-19 pandemic, are more akin to a defense lawyer's cross-examination of a cop who has the goods on the lawyer's guilty client, or a closing argument in support of their bosses' ideological beliefs that is presented with an air of self-righteous indignation and fairness, well practiced in the bathroom mirror. This state of affairs is bad under normal circumstances, but place it within a pandemic crisis, and it becomes an unmitigated disaster. Here is why.

When members of the general public believe, and for good reason, that virtually everything presented to them by the media entertainment complex is gamed, massaged, and motivated by partisan ideologies; when they realize that the people they voted into office are often motivated by their desire to exercise authority for authorities' sake and to preserve their job no matter what it takes, their mistrust can easily devolve to the point where they become unhinged from reality during events like COVID-19. This is especially true when people become scared and feel like they have little or no control. Sadly, the American public appears to prefer partisan theater posing as journalism over objective reportage—perhaps because they know nothing else.

People in a decompensated state of mind unconsciously distort reality in order to assuage their shredded nerves. It is not a coincidence that by coming to believe that the COVID-19 pandemic is not real, or certainly not as bad as government officials say it is, their fears are assuaged. Even believing that the government or some other unseen power created the COVID-19 pandemic makes people feel better, because at least some evil entity caused all of my fear, not an unseen, very real threat that cannot be easily controlled.

The unconscious dynamics at work provide solace through perceived control, e.g., "I could vote them out, or as the case may be, people could wake up and these evil people and forces couldn't have their way with us." People disconnected from a functionally literate understanding of infectious pathogens, who are meaningfully ignorant of what viruses are capable of, and who are plugged into social media where they glom onto people like themselves, construct scary castles in the sky, within which they take up residence, that make M.C. Escher's castles look like examples of classic architectural design. Such mindsets fueled by fears and coping defense mechanisms are heartbreaking to witness and have resulted in a clinical mental health disaster, piled on top of an already troubling medical and public health emergency.

People in authority who are notoriously controlling personality types at baseline come out of the woodwork and begin meddling in everything they can get their hands on during a national crisis. And as with all things they do, it is always for "the public's safety." This genre of politician, all too common in today's world, feels obligated to make daily public appearances that are often *painfully* transparent exercises in ego stroking and backslapping their political cronies' work. They are gleeful that now, more than ever, the hapless public can be put under their thumb—or so they think.

This behavior on the part of gleeful controllers in authority triggers fearful and suspicious people whose attitude toward people in authority is "I don't trust you" and "stay out of my life" during normal times. Independence and freedom are laudable ideals upon which the United States of America was founded. However, when confronted with a pandemic, a public that mistrusts their leaders, their medical advisors, and their media is not a good mix.

With all of the well-founded cynicism and doubts about what truly motivates politicians and the media entertainment complex to say and do what they do, the public is at a loss when it comes to COVID-19 and who to believe. Who do you trust? Where does the public look to for guidance? Well, ever since the advent of social media, they foolishly look to one another—and despite their doubts about the so-called fourth estate, they listen to **their** media darlings who know how to enrage, soothe, placate, and fuel their audience's natural tendency to engage in confirmation bias.

Enter the media personality whose stock in trade is to orient their sails in order to catch a thermal so they can increase their viewership, number of followers, friends, or Q-rating. I have chosen not to identify the following media personalities who have jumped on the COVID-19 thought leader bandwagon. The reason I have not identified them is that perhaps, upon reflection at a later date, these people who are in the tough business of pleasing their audience rather than educating them will reconsider their impact upon a public that is desperate for relief from the terror that is COVID-19.

Here is a tweet from a high-profile person with a rather large audience. I include this person's tweet because it reflects a common theme among some partisans with a particular ideological bent; but perhaps more importantly, it has encouraged members of the public who are inclined to resist hygienic public health guidelines at baseline to ramp up their resistance efforts.

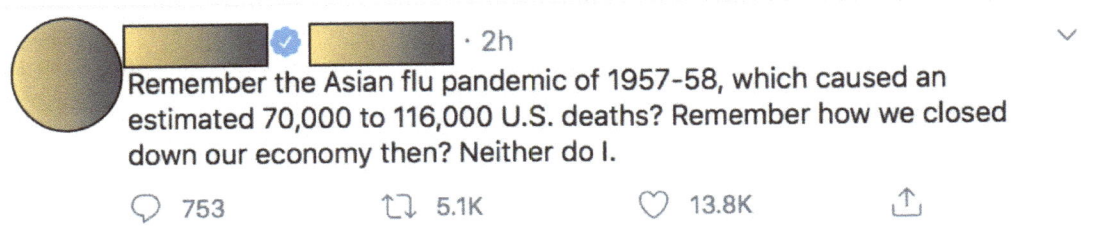

Take note of the fact that over 5,000 people retweeted this comment and nearly 14,000 people liked it. The point of the tweet is simply this: the Asian flu pandemic of 1957-58 [61] resulted in a lot of deaths (more than COVID-19 at the time of the tweet) yet federal and state governments back then didn't "close down the economy."

First of all, President Trump and his advisors chose to institute sweeping public health-related behavior restrictions in order to mitigate the empirically documented widespread death and illness that has resulted from each and every pandemic over the past century, including the Asian flu epidemic.

*The intent on the part of the government, especially President Trump, was **not** to close down the economy but to stem the course of the deadly SARS-CoV-2 virus—a distinction lost on many people. If you know nothing else, you should know that the President knew all too well that during an election year harming the economy by imposing strict public health guidelines would not be good for him—yet he did just that, albeit some of his critics say his response was untimely.*

Secondly, a number of exacerbating factors make SARS-CoV-2 exponentially more dangerous than the H2N2 virus that caused the Asian flu pandemic; thus, making any comparison between the two pathogens foolish at best, and at worst dangerously specious. President Trump and his advisors were confronted with a once-in-a-lifetime public health emergency.

As of May 25, 2020, approximately 100,000 people have died in the USA due to complications from having been infected with SARS-CoV-2, with that number still

---

[61] The Asian flu pandemic of 1957-58 actually took place between the years 1957 and 1963.

on the increase. The mid-range number of deaths from the Asian flu of 1957-58, between 70,000 and 116,000, comes out to 93,000 deaths. As of May 2020, the current population of the USA is:

United States Population (LIVE)

330,719,008

In 1955 the population of the USA was 171,685,336 people. By 1960 it had increased to 186,720,571. I'll take the mid-year's population of the USA during those census years for reference. That number works out to be: 179,202,954 people.

- Since 1957-58, the population has increased 84.5 percent, thereby increasing the number of people at risk for contracting the SARS-CoV-2 by that same percentage.

- In 1957-58, the number of international visitors coming into the USA was a fraction of what it is today in 2020. Approximately 500,000 international travelers entered the USA in 1958. In 2018, 79.2 million people entered the USA from overseas, with each person bringing with them their infectious pathogen payload.

- The infection potential of the H2N2 Avian virus when compared to the SARS-CoV-2 virus is like night and day. While direct comparisons have not been made due to the novelty of the SARS-CoV-2 virus, we know that the virus that causes COVID-19 is exponentially more contagious than the H2N2 virus. [62]

- The virulence of SARS-CoV-2 is without compare, including the H2N2 virus, when it comes to the severity of the syndromes it causes and its vexing symptom presentation. More and more troubling sequelae of SARS-CoV-2 are being discovered with each passing day, including a recently recognized

---

[62] Journal of Virology (2014) Jeremy C. Jones, Tatiana Baranovich, Bindumadhav M. Marathe, Angela F. Danner, Jon P. Seiler, John Franks, Elena A. Govorkova, Scott Krauss, and Robert G. Assessment of H2N2 Influenza Viruses from the Avian Reservoir. J Virol. 2014 Jan; 88(2): 1175–1188. doi: 10.1128/JVI.02526-13

deadly inflammatory syndrome that affects children, some as young as infants, referred to as pediatric multi-system inflammatory syndrome.[63]

Population and international travel increases from 1957-58 to 2020, along with the exponentially greater virulence and infection potential of the SARS-CoV-2 when compared to the H2N2, informs us that had President Trump and his advisors used our government's response to the 1957-58 Asian flu as a template for their response to COVID-19 in 2020, then rather than looking at a death toll as of mid-May 2020 of approximately 100,000 deaths, we would be grappling with the reality that a half-million or more people would have lost their lives by May 2020. Our death toll estimates are purposefully conservative, almost to a fault, to leave no room for an estimate that would miss on the top. President Trump has estimated millions of lives have been saved by the stringent public health behavioral modifications his administration put into place, to wit:

> "Think of the number — potentially 2.2 million people if we did nothing, if we didn't do the distancing, if we didn't do all of the things that we're doing." [64]

I think a lesson that jumps out at the objective observer is that our government's response to the 1957-58 Asian flu pandemic compared to President Trump and his medical advisor's response to the COVID-19 pandemic suggests that public health officials in the late 50s and early 60s abrogated their duty to protect American citizens.

Here is another media personality who voiced an opinion that strict public health restrictions are illogical and inconsistent, because as a society we don't invoke similar restrictions in other public health-related matters where there is loss of life.

> *"The fact of the matter is we have people dying, 45,000 people a year die from automobile accidents, 480,000 from cigarettes, 360,000 a year from swimming pools, but we don't shut the country down for that, but*

---

[63] New York State Department of Health: https://www.health.ny.gov/press/releases/2020/docs/2020-05-06_covid19_pediatric_inflammatory_syndrome.pdf
[64] President Trump: White House COVID-19 Briefing. April 26, 2020.

> *yet we're doing it for this? And the fallout is going to last for years because people's lives are being destroyed."*

So, let's compare apples to apples using this media personality's points of reference:

- Drowning deaths: A child who tragically drowns in a backyard swimming pool doesn't mean that the FTD delivery person who drops off a "condolences bouquet" to that home will go home and drown in his pool. But that is exactly what can happen with COVID-19.
- Death from cigarettes: Perhaps this person hasn't noticed, but government imposed restrictions on who, where, and when a person can smoke make social distancing guidelines look like kissing contest rules. Those smoking restrictions, just like those imposed by President Trump and his medical advisors in response to COVID-19, have saved hundreds of thousands, if not well over one million lives and countless bouts with severe illness, not to mention millions of dollars saved in health care costs.
- Automobile deaths: What if merely walking through a lot full of parked cars meant you could end up in the ICU? That can happen with SARS-CoV-2.

Our next media person shared with their audience their aversive emotional response to one particular public health edict; namely, the wearing of facemasks. To wit:

> *"I will never wear a mask with a political message on it. I will never wear a mask that has a team logo on it. And the reason for this is simple. The mask represents my imprisonment. The mask is the shackle, handcuff. There's nothing funny or cute or fashionable about the mask."*

I agree, the mask is not funny, cute or fashionable, it is much more meaningful—it saves lives. For a year and a half, I wore a surgical mask into surgery four times a week and never once felt like I was being oppressed because my surgeon supervisor refused to permit me to even enter the atrium of the surgical theater without a surgical mask. Nor did I have an aversive emotional response when it was demanded of me that I scrubbed continuously for 5 minutes before entering the surgical theater, even though I wasn't the one doing surgery. As far as glamorizing or adding your own aesthetic touches to a surgical mask, is that a bad thing? Many ER doctors in children's hospitals, along with nurses and support staff, wear fun scrubs and masks because it lightens things up. Would the wearing of a respirator still qualify as a form of imprisonment if the jailer were simply a deadly virus, and not a politician or bureaucrat who enjoys keeping people locked up?

I think media personalities often fail to be aware, don't care, or actually welcome that people who are terrified and feel that they have lost control are very impressionable and vulnerable. Moreover, many people have what we label an oppositional disorder. Oppositional disorder people resist and engage in obstructive behavior when they are ordered to do something, just like those people who suffer from paranoia often decompensate when secrecy is invoked.

Authoritarian parents gave us the gift of their children, who are obstreperous and now populate our thought leaders with their oppositional declarations—never stated as such, but always shrouded in the virtues of personal freedom and resistance to oppression. In the same way, many people in authority love imposing controls on their fellow man for control's sake. So it is that many people resist demands made upon them, whether or not a sound basis exists for those demands. Both personality types (Controlling and Oppositional), I might add, were molded by similar parenting styles.

Can we agree with the following revolutionary notion that people who engage in virus-friendly behavior are the real source of oppression, and not respirators, hand washing and social distancing? By the way, to those who feel imprisoned by public health guidelines based upon proven infectious disease facts: If you really want a taste of imprisonment, try on an intubation kit in the ICU...now that is imprisonment, not a lifesaving surgical mask with a happy smile on it.

I regret to conclude that many people, without reference to any of our quoted media personalities, put their spit-wet finger into the wind like a golfer assessing what club to use and concluded that it would be a good move to hop on the *resist the public health guidelines bandwagon*. For those who would label our analysis here somewhat cynical in that regard, we offer to you the words of George Bernard Shaw:

> *"The power of accurate observation is called cynicism by those who haven't got it."*

I encourage thought leaders to consider a few other matters of import before they purposefully or unwittingly encourage the general public to return to their normal way of doing things. The American public's nominal public health behaviors were remarkably virus-friendly leading up to the COVID-19 pandemic. As a result, the President and his medical advisors were virtually forced to impose strict public health guidelines, lest our country and the world face another 1918 pandemic. I also encourage those members of the public who listen to these thought leaders to swallow a bolus of this old saw: "Caveat emptor."

If the issue on the table is: "At what point in the course of a pandemic do public health officials lessen restrictions?" The answer is, "It depends." In the case of the USA, draconian restrictions were implemented out of necessity because of our premorbid, virus-friendly public health behavior. Once responsible public health behaviors were adopted by and/or imposed upon the public, we witnessed the expected flattening of the curve of new infections, soon followed by a reduction in death rates. However, these restrictions, which mandated social isolation, resulted in practically unavoidable serious mental health and economic side effects.

Almost all people find social isolation stressful; but for some, social isolation can push them over the edge. Common parlance has taken note of this psychological reaction to social isolation, e.g., "cabin fever" and "stir crazy." The social media content I have reviewed is both disturbing and heart-wrenching. Social media people who have never treated a patient started acting like a package of *Dr. Sea Monkey* eggs sprinkled into tepid water when COVID-19 hit. The ever-present social media personality gamer is the most disturbing, however, because they view their fellow humans' fear and neediness as an opportunity to exploit them in any way possible.

The economic ramifications of social isolation mandates can cause extreme stress when people are confronted with the loss of income and/or the loss of their business. Our identities are intertwined with our vocations and economic wellbeing. Business insolvency, bankruptcy, or simply having to undergo belt tightening can result in anxiety, depression, and in some people with certain predispositions, suicidal ideation or worse. Therefore, pandemic control, when viewed through a public health policy prism, becomes a balancing act between flattening the infection curve and protecting mental and economic health.

The key to making this balancing act work requires public health behavior to undergo a paradigm shift. Before COVID-19, nominal public health behavior in the USA was virus-friendly. A paradigm shift will have taken place when nominal public health behavior is pathogen-aversive and is enforced by the dynamic of social conformity, without the need for government mandates.

> ***We have made the case throughout this report that draconian public health edicts, as many characterize them, would have never been necessary in the first place if our nominal public health-related behaviors were less pathogen-friendly at baseline.***

Perhaps the most important reason we need a paradigm shift at this time in the course of COVID-19 is related to what infectious disease experts have known for a long time—viral pandemics come in sets of waves.

> ***However, unlike earthquakes that also tend to come in sets of waves, a virus-caused pandemic's aftershock, unlike a real earthquake, can be much higher on the Richter scale.***

With regard to pandemic waves, we took note of the fact that the Asian flu pandemic of 1957-58 actually lasted until 1963, when the last infection wave set took place. Take a look at the aftershocks of four different viral pandemics. These data are important, because when governments prematurely remove stringent anti-viral public health guidelines, they may reasonably expect a spike in infections and death.

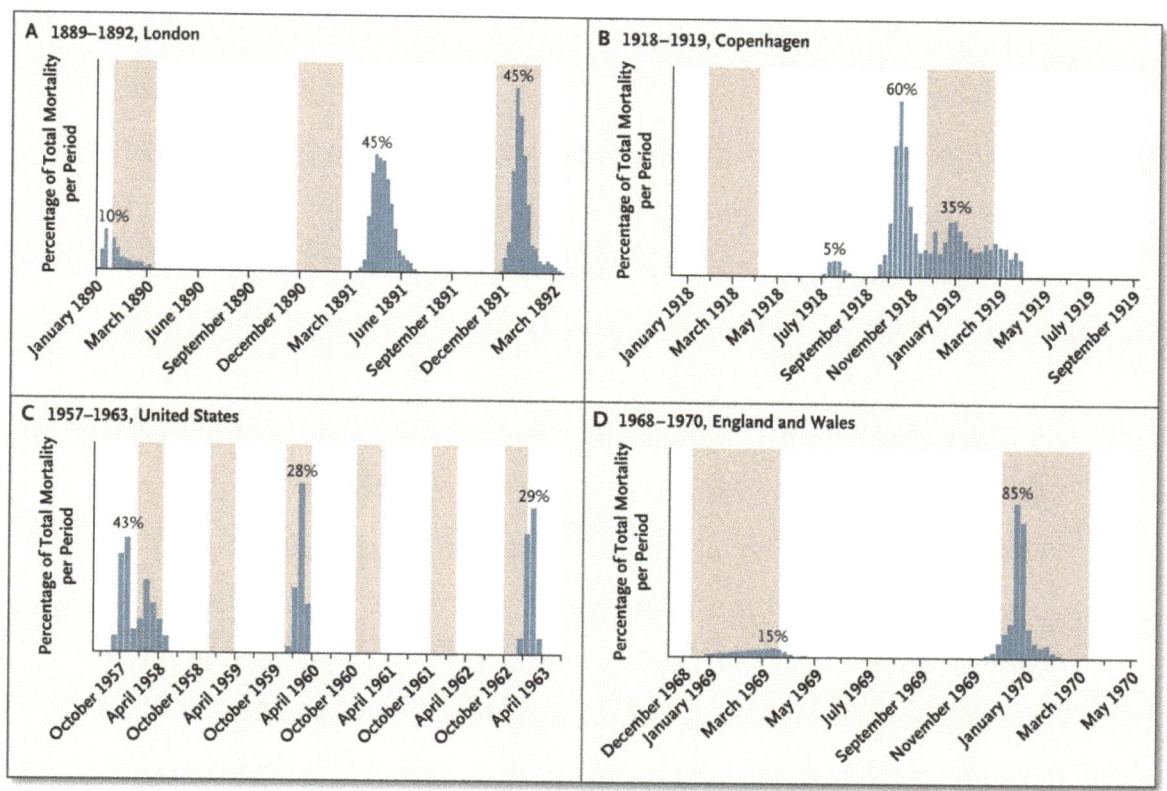

The Signature Features of Influenza Pandemics — Implications for Policy [65]

I would be remiss if I were to ignore the media entertainment complex's across-the-board criticisms of President Trump's alleged languid and untimely response to COVID-19. Depending upon who you read, listen to or believe, President Trump ignored numerous expert warnings about the seriousness of the soon-to-become pandemic in lieu of relying upon his gut that things would work out and be okay.

He Could Have Seen What Was Coming: Behind Trump's Failure on the Virus

"WASHINGTON — "Any way you cut it, this is going to be bad," a senior medical adviser at the Department of Veterans Affairs, Dr. Carter Mecher, wrote on the night of Jan. 28, in an email to a group of public health experts scattered around the government and universities. "The projected size of the outbreak already seems hard to believe."

A week after the first Coronavirus case had been identified in the United States, and six long weeks before President Trump finally took aggressive action to confront the danger the nation was facing — a

---

[65] Mark A. Miller, M.D., Cecile Viboud, Ph.D., Marta Balinska, Ph.D., and Lone Simonsen, Ph.D. (2009) N Engl J Med 2009; 360:2595-2598 DOI: 10.1056/NEJMp0903906.

pandemic that is now forecast to take tens of thousands of American lives — Dr. Mecher was urging the upper ranks of the nation's public health bureaucracy to wake up and prepare for the possibility of far more drastic action. "You guys made fun of me screaming to close the schools," he wrote to the group, which called itself "Red Dawn," an inside joke based on the 1984 movie about a band of Americans trying to save the country after a foreign invasion. "Now I'm screaming, close the colleges and universities." His was hardly a lone voice. Throughout January, as Mr. Trump repeatedly played down the seriousness of the virus and focused on other issues, an array of figures inside his government — from top White House advisers to experts deep in the cabinet departments and intelligence agencies — identified the threat, sounded alarms and made clear the need for aggressive action.

The president, though, was slow to absorb the scale of the risk and to act accordingly, focusing instead on controlling the message, protecting gains in the economy and batting away warnings from senior officials. It was a problem, he said, that had come out of nowhere and could not have been foreseen."[66]

Kaiser Health News published this headline:

Was The Novel Coronavirus Really Sneaky In Its Spread To The U.S.? Experts Say No.

["T]he alarm was sounded in January," said Jennifer Kates, a global health expert at the Kaiser Family Foundation. "This wasn't a surprise."

At that point, researchers told us, decisive and widespread federal action could have made a big difference. But publicly, Trump was still comparing the Coronavirus to the flu, downplaying the risk on Twitter

---

[66] New York Times. *He Could Have Seen What Was Coming: Behind Trump's Failure on the Virus.* By: Eric Lipton, David E. Sanger, Maggie Haberman, Michael D. Shear, Mark Mazzetti and Julian E. Barnes. April 11, 2020

and television, and declaring repeatedly that the new virus was under control." [67]

Whenever I witness "Monday morning quarterbacking," I reflexively reflect upon the words of the late Senator Sam Ervin (D) from North Carolina, who presided over the Senates' Watergate Hearings in 1973:

"People are like lightning bugs...they carry their illumination behind them."

That is not to say that Monday morning quarterbacks are necessarily incorrect, it only means that, as is often said in response to a joke that falls flat—"you had to be there."

For at least the last 50 years, virologists have been telling anyone who would listen that it is only a matter of time before one of these CoVs pulls a mutation out of the hat; a mutation then we'd be off to the races. It reminds me of the joke about an elderly married man who went to see a priest to confess the fact that over the past ten years, he has engaged in one extramarital affair after another with women less than half his age. When asked by his priest if he feels remorse over his sinful behavior, the elderly man said, "No, of course not." The priest then asked him, "Why did you come to confession to tell me?" To which the elderly man replied, "Hey, I'm telling everybody."

The problem is few people in charge ever listen to dire warnings regarding infectious diseases, no matter how solid the science, because of politics. For those who still believe in chauvinistic partisan politics litmus tests, when it comes to infectious diseases, i.e., Democrats v. Republicans, for the last 50 years every President, regardless of political affiliation, has been warned in no uncertain terms that it is only a matter of time before the next pandemic hits and that ***now is the time to prepare.*** Democrats, Republicans, Independents, one and all, displayed the same genuine response of concern to those warnings, not unlike the response of a parent to their child who tells them their first "why did the chicken cross the road"

---

[67] Kaiser Health News. Was The Novel Coronavirus Really Sneaky In Its Spread To The U.S.? Experts Say No. By: Shefali Luthra, March 19, 2020.

joke. You pretend you've never heard the joke before, and you laugh out of politeness because you know the child is sincere, but you've heard it all before.

When President Trump's senior infectious disease advisors, Drs. Anthony Fauci and Deborah Birx, stood before the press, the questions they faced were predictable both in tone and substance. When the good doctors agreed with the President or validated a previous statement made by him, they were subjected to insolent and loaded questions, e.g., "Are you afraid to answer the question honestly for fear of losing your job?" On the other hand, when Drs. Birx or Fauci said anything in whole or in part that could, if it were folded like a piece of paper in the hands of an origami expert, be used to ridicule and or undermine the president, the media entertainment complex had their booking agents on the phone with the good doctors in 30 minutes.

Serving in the role of infectious disease advisor to any politician, especially one that is the object of abject hatred by the media entertainment complex, is like walking a balance beam over a moat filled with crocodiles. A social media intoxicated public, conditioned to act exactly like the formal media entertainment complex it purportedly hates, engages in the same level of vilification or adoration depending upon which quote or part thereof can be used to put the maraschino cherry on top of their confirmation bias sundae, or to knock it off the dining room table onto the floor. Is it any wonder our best minds stay clear of politics, while those best minds that do brave the waters are tortured for helping?

Political theater aside, I'm much more interested in why the United States of America was so woefully unprepared when it came to ventilators, respirators, hospital beds, and a surprisingly inadequate stockpile of any number of medical necessities. Politicians who make the call to arms before a shot has been fired know that such a call will have little or no purchase power with a public that doesn't want to hear that the big one is coming when things are going good. It is like this: why fix a leaky roof when the sun is shining? Politicians busy sending as much money as they can siphon off from budget coffers to send back to their own districts, so as to insure their reelection, view tax revenue as a zero-sum game. They simply are not interested in allocating money in preparation for the next pandemic when that same money can go to one of their pet projects and guarantee their reelection in the process. If critical pharmaceuticals can be made in China at a lower cost and things are working out just fine, then why alienate a big campaign contributor?

Notwithstanding political motivations to downplay the seriousness of SARS-CoV-2 infections, most people simply don't comprehend and/or are in a state of denial as to where they fit into the pathogen as predator taxonomy. To know the truth is a sobering realization—but from that realization can come some degree of clarity.

When it comes to this boxing card's main event: Virulent Pathogens v. The People of the World, the pathogens are Muhammad Ali in his prime and the rest of us, no matter how smart or tough, are little more than a "Tomato Can." [68]

National Security and Pathogen Friendly Public Health Behavior

I have repeatedly referenced the tendency to game any national tragedy, including pandemics, for personal and/or ideological gain. The examples I have given up to this point have been linear and intuitive in nature. What I have not discussed involves the more sophisticated and counterintuitive tactics and strategies used by well-funded political and ideological interests to exploit pandemics for political and ideological advantage.

Pandemics often create a perfect storm environment where social contracts may be weakened or shattered. Social contracts are the glue that holds civil society together. Pandemics create a perfect storm environment because of their negative impact upon mental and physical health and the destructive impact upon economies. A weakened economy and a citizenry under great stress are perceived as harvestable vulnerabilities by vested

---

[68] In boxing, kickboxing or mixed martial arts, "tomato can" is an idiom for a fighter with poor or diminished skills (at least when compared with the opponent they are placed against).

interests that have been waiting for just the right time to deliver a body blow to their adversaries.

Just as an arsonist needs a spark to ignite a devastating fire, ideological arsonists need a trigger event to set fire to an emotionally exhausted populace and an economy that has been weakened by a pandemic. Politicians not up to the job may not have the wherewithal to counter such ideological coups. In fact, they may not even recognize them as such because of their own psychological defenses. To make matters even more dangerous during times of pandemic, ideologically driven politicians hostile to existing social contracts welcome if not facilitate trigger events. In that situation, we may count on the fact that this genre of politician will stand by as if helpless or in some instances actually inflame manufactured upheavals once fires have been set.

From a military intelligence perspective, the number of dominoes between a virulent community pathogen, a virus-friendly public health norm and an attempt at a coup d'état is only three. All that it takes to knock these three dominoes down is a trigger event. This sobering state of affairs means that people in charge of a nation under siege by a pandemic must be acutely aware that their adversaries, both foreign and domestic, view them as ripe for exploitation and will actively search out and audition trigger events. If a trigger event does not spontaneously occur, then a manufactured one can be generated with relative ease.

Trigger events possess both tangible and symbolic value with the two not mutually exclusive from one another. Some trigger events are weighted toward the tangible impact they have while others are predominantly symbolic in nature. Trigger events weighted more toward the material end of the spectrum include such things as hurricanes, earthquakes and wild fires. Trigger events weighted more toward the symbolic end of the spectrum include singular events that, though they may be personally tragic, strike a chord with a critical mass number of people. Examples of this genre of trigger event include assassinations of political or race identity leaders, police officers that harm otherwise unarmed or innocent people who belong to a category of an aggrieved demographic or judicial outcomes that prove in the minds of an aggrieved demographic the existence of a structural injustice that applies to them.

The reason trigger events work so well within the context of a pandemic is the same reason that torching a pile of oily rags is guaranteed to set them ablaze. Pandemics tend to deplete people of their emotional reserves to the point where they are easily triggered. Once triggered, their frustrations, fears and pent-up anger may erupt in acts of mass violence — sometimes to the point of anarchy.

During pandemics, where stay-at-home orders have been imposed, people have a lot of idle time on their hands. People with time on their hands, especially those who have been provided government subsidies and who also feel aggrieved as a nominal state of mind, in keeping with our analogy, constitute a pile of rags soaked in gasoline just waiting for a tangible or symbolic trigger event to set them ablaze. Keep in mind that social media allows provocateurs to organize at the drop of hat, so mass existential angst can be transformed into violent mobs with a few swipes on a smart phone within hours after a trigger event has occurred.

Absent an organic trigger event, synthetic versions are relatively easy to generate. AstroTurf trigger events are an art form whose practitioners write their PhD dissertations on how to socially engineer them like some people engineer virulent viruses in their labs that look organic. By the way, the best synthetic trigger events are those that are virtually indistinguishable from organic trigger events in the same way that some lab-created diamonds are virtually indistinguishable from the real thing.

Nevertheless, a number of tells give away the etiology of mass uprisings and their trigger events. Interestingly, one of those tells applies equally well to mass upheavals and diamonds. Some lab-created diamonds are too perfect when compared to the real thing, thus giving them away as fake. Organic upheavals have a spontaneous, if not messy quality to them, not unlike the work of a sloppy weekend warrior house painter with all the splatters, spills and paint on the painter we expect to see. On the other hand, synthetic upheavals look very much like the handiwork of a team of professional house painters that work as a coordinated unit with paint applied exactly where it belongs with just the right brush even though these alleged house painters are portrayed by the media as amateurs. The terms "fanning the flames" and "throwing gasoline on a fire" describe behavioral patterns that betray the handiwork of those who premeditatively exploit pandemics for ideological advantage.

But one tell has been the gold standard for a very long time when it comes to distinguishing between organic and socially engineered trigger events. *When trigger events show up at just the right time, with the perfect cast of characters who execute their plans with surgical precision, people in the intelligence community always ask this question: "Why this, why now and who stands to gain?"*

When is the perfect time to engineer a trigger event within the context of a pandemic? It is that point in time when the affected country's infection and death rate curves begin to flatten and show signs of returning to normal. Who knew that a public's pathogen-friendly public health behavior is a national security issue? Everyone with a hostile agenda who has access to practitioners of socially engineered coup d'états, that's who.

How to Play Russian Roulette with Viruses

Every time a virus smuggles its DNA or RNA into its hosts' cells, it plays a game of Russian roulette with its own genetic blueprint, because it turns over control of its own replication to another species' copying machinery. SARS-CoV-2 happens to be an RNA virus.⁶⁹ Regardless, the replication process would apply equally to DNA-based viruses, but for some highly technical differences.⁷⁰ Viruses use their host's machinery to assemble nucleic acids to make copies of themselves. Such is the nature of all viruses, because they have no replication machinery of their own.

SARS-CoV-2 is comprised of 29,881 nucleotides. Each one of those nucleotides has to be faithfully copied, and the sequence of these building blocks must be maintained in order to create a carbon copy of the virus. Sometimes mistakes are made. These mutations, as we refer to them, may result in a difference without functional effect. Sometimes they can weaken the virus, or sometimes such mutations can create a Frankenstein virus, one that can enter its host without its host's immune system even knowing that it is there. In the case of HIV, this virus attacks the immune system of its host, a tactic that military strategists use in modern air combat where the first air strikes are made against the air defenses of the target. While we are talking about HIV, let's broach the topic at hand, because how HIV came to cause so much misery and death can be laid at the doorstep of human behavior, to wit:

> *HIV crossed from chimps to humans in the 1920s in what is now the Democratic Republic of Congo. This was probably as a result of chimps carrying the Simian Immunodeficiency Virus (SIV), a virus closely related to HIV, being **hunted and eaten by people living in the area**.* ⁷¹

---

[69] Ribonucleic acid (RNA) is a polymeric molecule essential in various biological roles in coding, decoding, regulation and expression of genes. RNA and DNA are nucleic acids and along with lipids, proteins and carbohydrates, constitute the four major macromolecules essential for all known forms of life.

[70] DNA viruses utilize its hosts' cell proteins and enzymes to make additional DNA that is transcribed to messenger RNA (mRNA), which is then used to direct protein synthesis. RNA viruses usually use the RNA core as a template for synthesis of viral genomic RNA and mRNA. The viral mRNA directs the host cell to synthesize viral enzymes and capsid proteins, and to assemble new virions. Of course, there are exceptions to this pattern. If a host cell does not provide the enzymes necessary for viral replication, viral genes supply the information to direct synthesis of the missing proteins. Retroviruses, such as HIV, have an RNA genome that must be reverse transcribed into DNA, which then is incorporated into the host cell genome.

[71] Gao, F. et al (1999) 'Origin of HIV-1 in the chimpanzee Pan troglodytes troglodytes' Nature 397(6718): 436-441.

We all know someone who has been ravaged by the HIV virus. The world economic impact of HIV is estimated to be in the billions, if not trillions, of dollars, and all because certain inhabitants of the Congo *like* to eat chimpanzees. They don't *have* to eat chimpanzees, no. They *like* to hunt and eat them.

Now just think for a moment, if the relatively few chimpanzees hunted and killed because some Congolese *like* to eat them resulted in the scourge of AIDS, what would you say to someone who came up with the idea of purposefully raising tens of millions of chimpanzees in facilities where, by necessity, they were bred and kept in such numbers that their natural virus replication strategies were amped up as if on anabolic steroids to replicate with abandon, until they had their throats slit, hoisted up by their legs where they would bleed out onto factory floors and where their cut-up parts were sold to people all over the world who just *loved*, didn't *need*, but *loved* the taste of chimpanzee meat. Imagine if these "chimp killers" paid off the politicians who regulated them and paid the media entertainment complex tens of millions of dollars to advertise, that is SELL, their chimp meat to the average person. You'd have celebrities sitting down with their beautiful spouse, consuming juicy chimp meat, and you'd have actors blessed with mellifluous voices read the line: "Chimp, it's what's for dinner."

What would you think if human beings actually did such a thing as a matter of common practice with pigs, chickens, cows, and other living creatures, given what you have learned from this book about how viruses replicate and spawn lethal versions of themselves? And to be sure, it doesn't take millions upon millions of so-called food animals to be raised by humans for bad things to happen—so imagine how bad the current situation is in the world, given that we do roll the dice with abandon given our food choices.

Go back 100 years to the state of Kansas in the USA.[72] This is where we find farmers involved in the business of breeding, raising, and then slaughtering pigs, cows, chickens, and other animals as their way to make money. At least one of these

---

[72] The current author has concluded that Kansas was the source of the 1918 pandemic that killed from 20 to 40 million people based upon statistical analysis. Nevertheless, informed analysts have identified Great Britain, France, or China as the ground zero location. Regardless, the Spanish Flu of 1918, as it is most frequently called, did **not** originate in Spain.

doomed creatures housed a replicating virus we have come to label the H1N1 virus. That virus jumped to one of the farmers who bred, raised, and then killed the so-called "food animal," who then spread his or her deadly virus payload to other unsuspecting humans.

> *"No one knows for sure what farm, what family may have first fallen ill. The community was most likely Santa Fe, now a ghost town in Haskell County," says Darlene Groth, curator at Haskell County Historical Society in Sublette. What is known is that a Kansas country doctor — Dr. Loring Miner, who practiced in Haskell County — became concerned when he noticed this three-day flu wasn't typical. It was an "influenza of the severe type," he wrote, and hit young, strong and otherwise healthy people the hardest. He was the first to report to Public Health Reports —a publication of the U.S. Public Health Service — that this flu was a killer. Dr. Miner could not have known that a perfect storm of circumstances was developing to rapidly spread the virus around the world. At any point, it could have lost its potency. But it didn't — it kept building in strength like a wildfire each time large groups of people were forced into crowded situations in geographic centers around the world.* [73]

Humans, never at a loss to throw fuel on an already raging fire, became embroiled in World War I, which also began in 1918. These same infected farm boys who unwittingly manufactured the H1N1, without any awareness whatsoever, were drafted into service and reported for duty at Fort Riley.

> *"Camp Funston, at Fort Riley, was the largest training facility in the Army, full of makeshift non-insulated barracks, housing 250 soldiers each. It teemed with soldiers from all over the Midwest, training for duty in France. They trained over 50,000 troops at a time who all lived in close quarters. The Army was cognizant that it needed to help our French and British Allies out, so there was no questioning, they were*

---

[73] Wichita Eagle (February 19, 2018) By: Becky Tanner: How a killer flu spread from western Kansas to the world.

sending troops out — soldiers were being sent that had flu-like symptoms," said Robert Smith, supervisory curator for Fort Riley Museums. Troops traveled by train from the Midwest to ports, then boarded ships bound for the war. "Recruits were being shifted from camp to camp by the thousands and they were taking with them fatigue and it made for easy exposure. The infections and disease followed," Smith said. Along the way, the virus mutated, many times. It hit people in waves, becoming more virulent each time. The first wave in the winter of 1918 was serious. The second wave — during the summer, when many of the soldiers were on the Western Front — was deadly, Smith said. The third wave came during the fall, when troops were returning. "We gave it to our Allies and they gave it to our enemies," Smith said. The virus mutated along the way as men coughed and sneezed, spreading germs in Army barracks, then on trains across the nation and on ships to Europe. Within six to nine months, the 1918 influenza pandemic had killed at least 20 million people worldwide. Some reports said 40 million. [74]

For readers who labor under the specious belief that the current crop of politicians invented the behavioral restrictions put in place in the spring of 2020 in order to mollify the spread of SARS-CoV-2 or, in some minds, cripple the world's economy or similar motivation, I share this bit of history with you compiled by the prescient and brilliant work of Becky Tanner, writing for the Wichita Eagle:

In early October of 1918, Dr. Samuel Crumbine, secretary of the state board of health, issued a statewide shutdown order to stop the spread of the disease. Visitors were barred from all state institutions, movie theaters were closed, and local authorities were told to discontinue public meetings. People were advised to keep their feet dry and try not to get chilled. Churches, schools, theaters were closed. In Goessel, members of the Alexanderwohl Mennonite Church held funeral services

---

[74] Ibid.

outside the building for the flu victims in an attempt to avoid spreading the disease. The Wichita Eagle published homework assignments from teachers and sermons of local ministers. The Eagle reported that nearly 200 people died during October — more deaths in the city than had ever before been recorded in a single month.

Permit me to draw a couple of analogies for readers who may still not glean how their *personal* discretionary behavior is inextricably linked to the COVID-19 pandemic. Let's use a gambling analogy with an eye on probabilities. Let's take a naturally occurring lethal version of a virus that is the result of the viruses' naturally occurring mutations and compare that outcome to throwing snake eyes 20 times in a row. The chances of throwing snake eyes 20 times in a row are slim to none. However, we know from history that naturally occurring lethal viral mutations, even without industrialized human meddling, have resulted in scourges like the pandemic of 1918 and AIDS. Now just imagine for a moment if we modified the probabilities associated with creating lethal viral mutations in the same way we have modified stock trading when we invented computer programs that could trade millions of times a second, or password decryption programs that can generate a million password combinations in a matter of seconds.

Imagine hundreds of millions of dice throwers, and set them up in factory farms where each dice thrower throws their cubes 24 hours a day, 365 days per year nonstop, just as fast as the croupier can deliver their dice back to them for the next throw. Also, imagine if those dice were loaded. Those dice are loaded in the meat industry, where immunocompromised, antibiotic-drenched, overcrowded as in beak to beak, hoof to hoof, continuously stressed, and like all sentient beings, stressed; their endocrine systems flood their bodies with so many hormones that their flesh becomes a deadly cocktail for man, and a warm and inviting Petri dish for viruses. [75]

What do you think the odds would be that one (it only takes one) of those hundreds of millions of loaded dice throwers living in the midst of those rancid Petri

---

[75] For a basic review of this issue please read: https://www.vox.com/future-perfect/2020/4/22/21228158/coronavirus-pandemic-risk-factory-farming-meat.

dishes would throw snake eyes 20 times in a row; that is, create a deadly pandemic-capable virus? You might remark: "Well, too bad for the gambler." Not so fast. In this game of chance, even if you've never gambled once in your life, you are the loser. I've thoroughly documented herein that humans have been rolling loaded dice for the past 100 years when it comes to their food choices and their nominal public health behavior. Even after 50+ million deaths, millions of debilitating illnesses, and trillions of lost dollars to the economy, the general public still seems oblivious to the fact that their discretionary choices, including diet, are responsible for their own downfall, to wit:

Let's return to the Asian flu of the late 1950s. In February 1957, a new influenza A (H2N2) virus emerged in East Asia, triggering a pandemic ("Asian Flu") referred to earlier in this paper. This H2N2 virus was comprised of three different genes from an H2N2 virus that originated from an avian influenza A virus, including the H2 hemagglutinin and the N2 neuraminidase genes. It was first reported in Singapore in February 1957, Hong Kong in April 1957, and in coastal cities in the United States in summer 1957. The estimated number of deaths was 1.1 million worldwide and 116,000 in the United States. The source was found to be wild ducks, perhaps geese and domestic chickens used for food. Wild fowl appeared to be immune to the virus, but farmed chickens were not.

The 1968 pandemic was caused by the influenza A (H3N2) virus. Avian influenza virus H3N2 is endemic in pigs in China, and has been detected in pigs in Vietnam, fueling the emergence of new variant strains. The H3N2 virus is comprised of two genes from an avian influenza-A virus, including a new H3 hemagglutinin, but also contained the N2 neuraminidase from the 1957 H2N2 virus. It was first noted in the United States in September 1968. The estimated number of deaths was 1 million worldwide and about 100,000 in the United States. Most excess deaths were in people 65 years and older. The H3N2 virus continues to circulate worldwide as a seasonal influenza A virus. Seasonal H3N2 viruses, which are associated with severe illness in older people, undergo regular antigenic drift.

The 1997 H5N1 bird flu outbreak developed on Chinese chicken farms. This factory farm-engineered chicken virus mutated for the next five years, between 1997 and 2005, becoming more lethal with each iteration. By the late fall of 2006, there were 258 confirmed cases and 153 people dead, along with the one-time mass killing of a staggering 140 million chickens, just so people would have some degree of confidence that they could continue to eat the next 140 million chickens bred then butchered alive until these same operations would *inevitably* generate the next problem virus.

The 2009 H1N1 swine flu outbreak was engineered in a pig confinement operation in North Carolina. The U.S. Centers for Disease Control and Prevention (CDC) estimated there were 60.8 million cases, 274,000 hospitalizations and between 8,868 and 18,306 deaths. A million or more pigs were buried alive so as to keep the public confident enough to buy their next round of pork chops and bacon.

In 2015, yet another variation of the H5N1 avian flu, similar to the original 1997 avian flu, forced American poultry farmers to kill tens of millions of their chickens en masse, just so they could continue to breed then slaughter alive the next tens of millions of chickens so people could continue to eat what they *like* to eat, not what they *need* to eat. Enter the so-called wet market.

While not all stereotypical wet markets sell animals still breathing and conscious in small cages, waiting in fear as they observe their cell mates yanked from their cages to have their throats slit before gleeful-hungry onlookers, most wet markets do just that. All across the world, cats, dogs, pigs, chickens, and almost any other living creature that flies, swims, or walks on land can be seen shaking in utter terror waiting their turn for the next patron to utter the words: Wǒ yào nàgè, or that one looks fat. [76]

And while these so-called wet markets are small potatoes when compared to factory meat operations, they have become the focus of heightened attention because of COVID-19 and the fact that the American consumer seems oblivious to the fact that all meat processing is wet. Peruse photos of slaughterhouse kill floor workers and you will notice that all of them wear tall rubber wading-type boots.

---

[76] "I'll have that one." 我要那个

That is because the floors and surrounding areas are literally soaked with blood, urine, feces, and spit.

Before the reader points the finger solely at Asian culture, and to be sure stereotypical wet markets are more common there than anyplace else in the civilized world, e.g. the annual Yulin Dog Meat Festival in China:

Annual Dog and Cat Meat Festival in Yulin, China (New York Times)

Annual Dog and Cat Meat Festival in Yulin, China (New York Times)

The USA has its fair share of wet markets as well. In fact, ground central for America's COVID-19 pandemic, New York City, has its fair share of wet markets. This from the U.K.'s THE SUN, U.S. Edition [77]

---

[77] The SUN, U.S. Edition: 'Wet markets' with HUNDREDS of birds stuffed in cages to be slaughtered still open in NEW YORK despite outcry. By: Erin Van Der Meer, April 27, 2020.

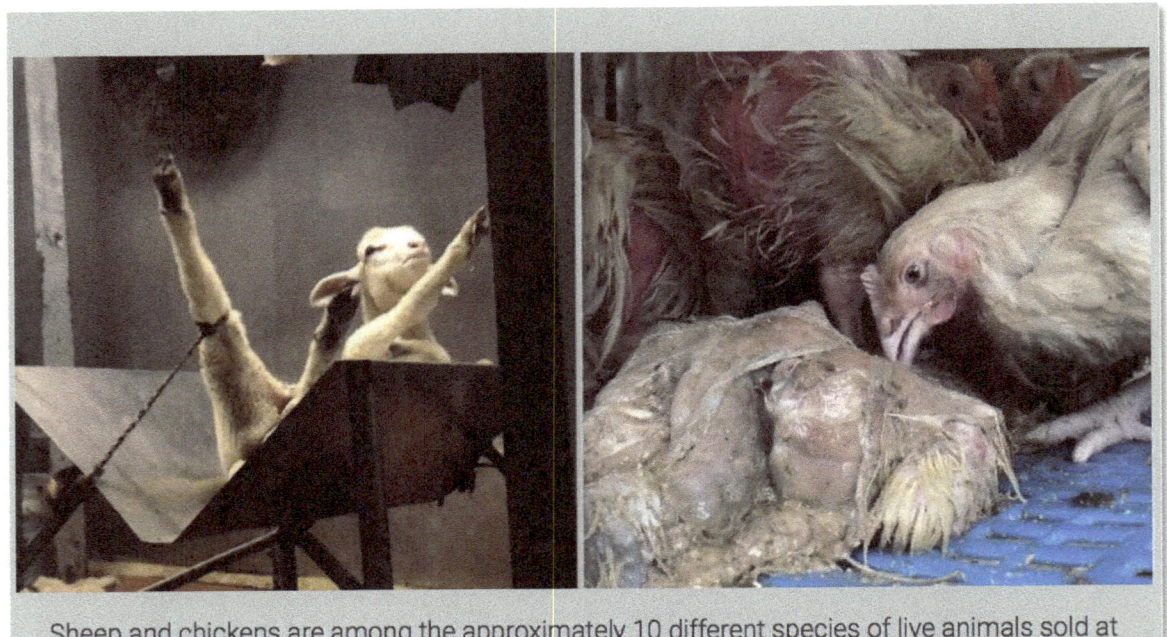

Sheep and chickens are among the approximately 10 different species of live animals sold at NYC's wet markets

I'm sure it is comforting to some readers to think that only certain kinds of animal markets are wet markets. As we have already alluded, all meat markets and meat sections in grocery stores are wet markets, merely once removed. The only distinction between the stereotypical wet markets pictured above, including the Huanan wet market, and the meat department in your grocery store, involves time, distance, scope and species of animal butchered alive; with the modern meat industry having no equal when it comes to the number of animals butchered alive and the concurrent pathogen amplification that results.

The major difference between the stereotypical Asian wet market and the meat section in the western world's supermarkets involves where, when and what animals are killed. What modern-day meat markets make up for in terms of food safety is more than offset by the huge numbers of animals continually slaughtered 24/7 in order to stock the shelves. While time and space disparities make no difference when comes to viruses, they constitute critically important psychological differences. The fact that animals are brutally killed in wet

factories far removed from where most people live makes it possible for consumers to enjoy the blind spot created by "out of sight, out of mind."

Please keep in mind as you peruse the following disturbing photographs that the author's purpose is not to shock the reader or proselytize a food ideology. In fact, I regret that I had no choice but to include the following photographs in order to drive home the point about pathogen amplification and the meat industry.

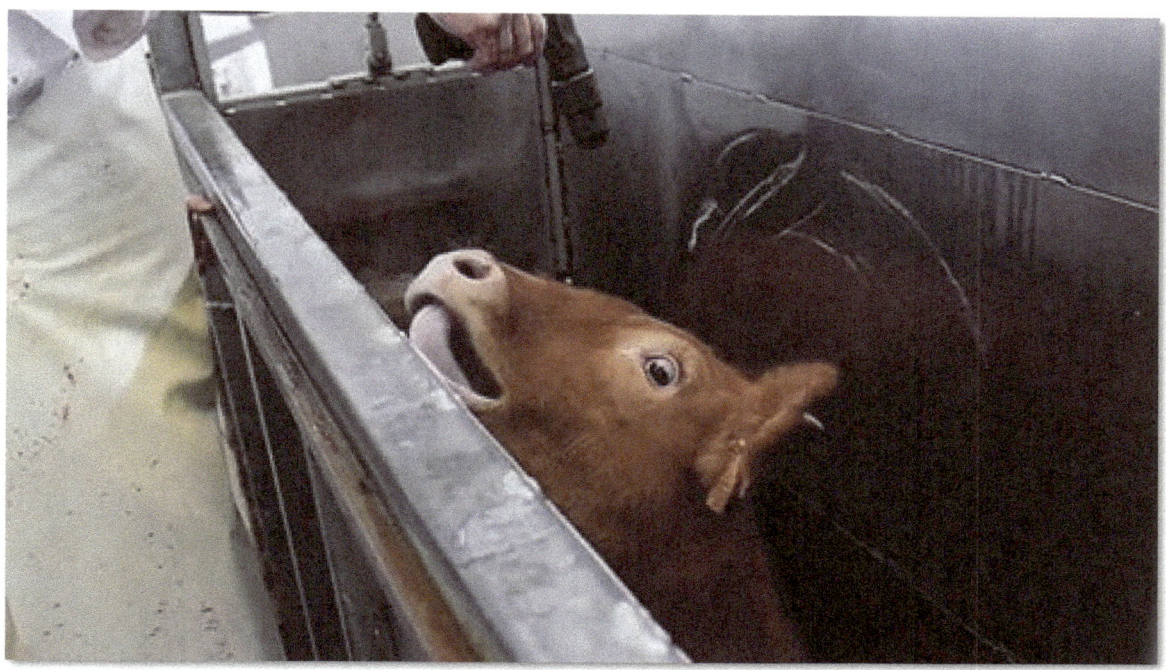

Preamble to Wet Calf Processing *(locations unidentified for security reasons)*

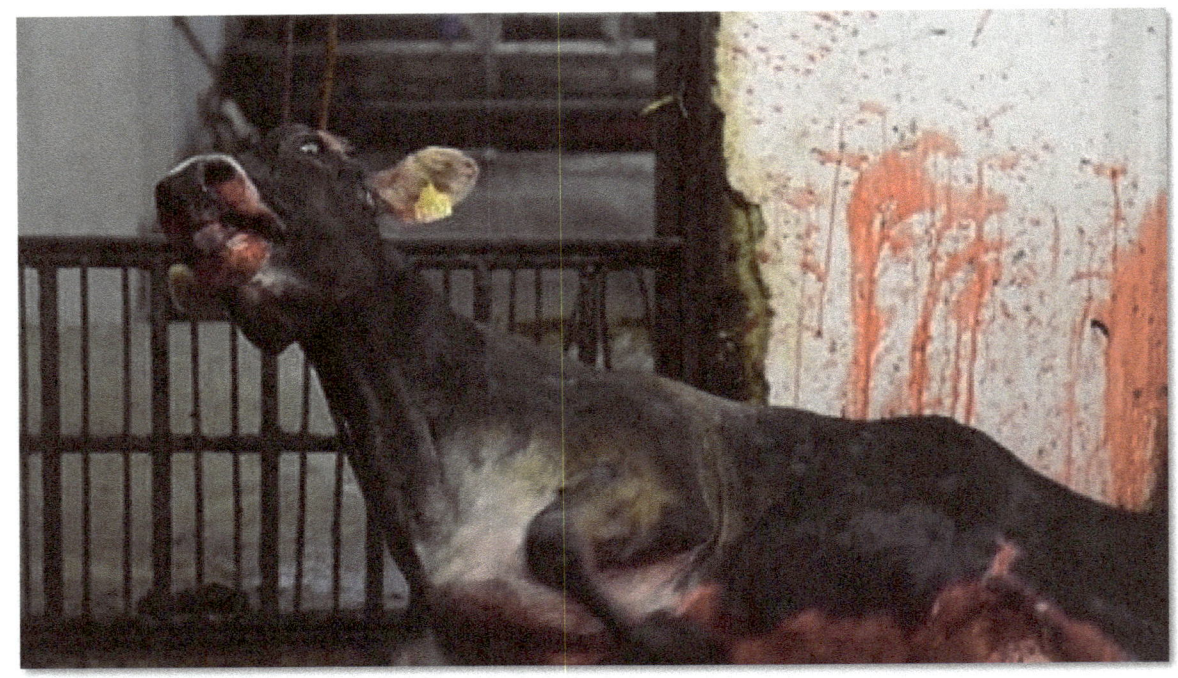

Wet Cow Processing *(locations unidentified for security reasons)*

The Wet Finished Product

Wet "Veal" (baby cows) Processing *(locations unidentified for security reasons)*

The Wet Finished Product

Pigs Waiting Their Turn to be Butchered Alive as Part of Wet Meat Processing *(locations unidentified for security reasons)*

For those readers whose out of sight, out of mind defenses are still intact or simply don't care, I suggest you buttress your psychological defenses, because if you have eaten bacon, among other animals since 2014, then you are a customer of the Chinese meat business. The largest pork producer in the entire world that breeds, fattens, and then slaughters pigs is owned lock, stock and barrel by the Chinese—home to Wuhan, Guangdong, the Huanan wet market, and the Wuhan Institute of Virology, as well as the home of countless virus outbreaks over the past 20 years.

Smithfield Foods, Inc., is located in Smithfield, Virginia. The WH Group of China owns the all-American sounding "Smithfield Foods."

206,657 views | Apr 16, 2020, 05:57pm EDT

The Chinese Billionaire Whose Company Owns Troubled Pork Processor Smithfield Foods

 **Jennifer Wang** Forbes Staff
Billionaires

Wan Long, Chairman and CEO of WH Group. (Photo by Nora Tam/South China Morning Post via Getty ... [+]   SOUTH CHINA MORNING POST VIA GETTY IMAGES

The Chinese own 500 farms in the USA under various American-sounding names, and another 2,000 independent farms around America where they breed, fatten, and then pay Americans to do the butchering alive. The Americans who kill animals for a living suffer from a hugely disproportionate number of serious mental illnesses, which costs millions of dollars in health care costs every year. What few observers ever mention are the smells and sounds of killing, particularly the sounds. Sentient beings have an acute awareness of their death, and like all sentient beings go into a fight-or-flight panic. The animals cry, scream, shake, go into panic breathing mode; they snort, gasp for air; they squeal and they cry real tears. If the humans near this have any functioning mirror neurons whatsoever,[78] their own death reactions kick in, which makes the entire process a recipe for mental illness. It appears that the only people not affected are psychopaths—when that is factored into the process, it adds an entirely new and very disturbing dimension to this horror show that has been repackaged and sold to the American public.

"The mental trauma of the first kill. Slaughter employees inevitably remember their first encounter with the slaughterfloor and having to slaughter. They recall vivid images of blood and describe the experience as traumatic, feeling overwhelmed by the immediate requirement to kill and the anticipation of having to slaughter hundreds of animals on the very first day. During their first kill, slaughter workers remember feeling upset and experiencing physical shock manifested by shaking and shivering. RP8 recalls: "When I shot my first animal, I started shaking" and RP10: "I was so scared, even when holding the gun, I was shaking." Slaughterfloor employees were also emotionally disturbed by their first-time kill and noted feeling pained, saddened, and shameful. In the words of RP9 reflecting on his first slaughter, the traumatic experience of the first kill is evident as well as how this emotive experience fades into detachment which is discussed as part of the (mal)adjustment phase."[79]

Referring back to playing Russian roulette with viruses, WH Group, as of 2006, bred and raised 15 million pigs a year and slaughtered over 27 million per year. In the heart of the conservative southern state of North Carolina, in Tar Heel, the Chinese own a 973,000 square-foot slaughter house where 32,000 living pigs

---

[78] A mirror neuron is a neuron that fires both when an animal acts and when the animal observes the same action performed by another. Thus, the neuron "mirrors" the behavior of the other, as though the observer was engaged in the action himself. Such neurons have been directly observed in primate species. Birds have been shown to have imitative resonance behaviors and neurological evidence suggests the presence of some form of mirroring system. In humans, brain activity consistent with that of mirror neurons has been found in the premotor cortex, the supplementary motor area, the primary somatosensory cortex, and the inferior parietal cortex.

[79] Karen Victor and Antoni Barnard (2016) *Slaughtering for a living: A hermeneutic phenomenological perspective on the well-being of slaughterhouse employees.* International Journal of Qualitative Studies on Health and Well-being.

are butchered alive EACH AND EVERY DAY. For my readers outside the USA, the Chinese have pig killing operations in Mexico, Poland, Romania, Germany, and the United Kingdom.

As part of the trade deal hammered out in 2019 between China and the United States, China now ships chickens it bred, raised, killed, and then cooked to the USA. Under the same trade deal worked out between the Trump administration and the Chinese, parts of cows slaughtered in China can now be sold in America. [80]

I don't want the reader to get the idea that pathogen amplification, which is part and parcel to the meat industry, is a Chinese, Asian, South American, or a select group of nation's problem—because it is not. The Chinese, in fact, all too familiar with the virus amplification that goes with meat farming regardless of where animals are slaughtered, **placed a ban on USA slaughtered chickens back in 2015** after America's avian virus outbreak of that same year. That ban was just lifted in 2019, to wit:

> **Poultry Stocks Take Wing With Lifting of China Import Ban**
>
> "Share prices of chicken producers have taken flight following China's
>
> lifting of a four-year old ban on importing poultry from the U.S." [81]

Ah, but these problems are solved by Kosher or Halal kills, you might remark. Think again please:

> **CDC finishes investigation of deadly outbreak traced to kosher chicken**
>
> *"Federal health officials say they have concluded their investigation into a deadly 11-month Salmonella outbreak associated with chicken from Empire Kosher. Twenty-five people from six states were confirmed infected and one person died, according to the Dec. 7 outbreak from the Centers for Disease Control and Prevention. Ill people ranged in age from less than one year to 76 years old. The patients' illness onset dates range from Sept. 25, 2017, through Aug. 13, 2018. The outbreak strain*

---

[80] Open Markets Institute. Meatpacking More Dangerous Today Than a Generation Ago, Amplifying COVID-19 Crisis. By: Claire Kelloway in Newsletter, Resiliency, Slaughterhouse Labor.
[81] Wall Street Journal, October 31, 2019. By: Kirk Maltais and Ryan Dezember.

of Salmonella I 4,[5],12:i: was particularly virulent, with half of the patients requiring hospitalization." [82]

What about Halal? The following is from the publication FOOD POISONING BULLETIN dated May 22, 2020:

- Salmonella Jouni Meats and Gab Halal Ground Beef Outbreak Sickens 22
- Halal Beef Producer Indicted Halal Manti Beef Dumplings Recalled for Lack of Inspection
- Baraka Bakery Recalls Halal Ground Beef for Possible E. coli

If your takeaway from this cursory review of documented pathogen generation as part of the meat industry is "there are no exceptions," then you drew an accurate conclusion.

It is crystal clear that governments and meat farmers know the pathogen-based and other health risks their operations pose to consumers and their workers in their native and export destined countries more than consumers know the risks. As you will learn, however, the public can be excused somewhat for their ignorance and food choices, because they were conditioned to eat what they have been fed by some of the most manipulative and amoral people on earth. *Moreover, mind controllers created in their victims something that if it were not so malevolent would be awe-inspiring. They actually managed to motivate their victims to:*

> **Defend their self-destructive and horrendously cruel food selections as if those choices are a religion and/or act of Jeffersonian courage in the face of an anti-American Communist regime. Tens of millions of infectious pathogen related deaths and unfathomable cruelty? No problem—and here is why.**

Before I begin this next set of narratives I want to remind the reader of an apropos quote from the great Mark Twain:

---

[82] Food Safety News. CDC finishes investigation of deadly outbreak traced to kosher chicken. By: Coral Beach, December 8, 2018.

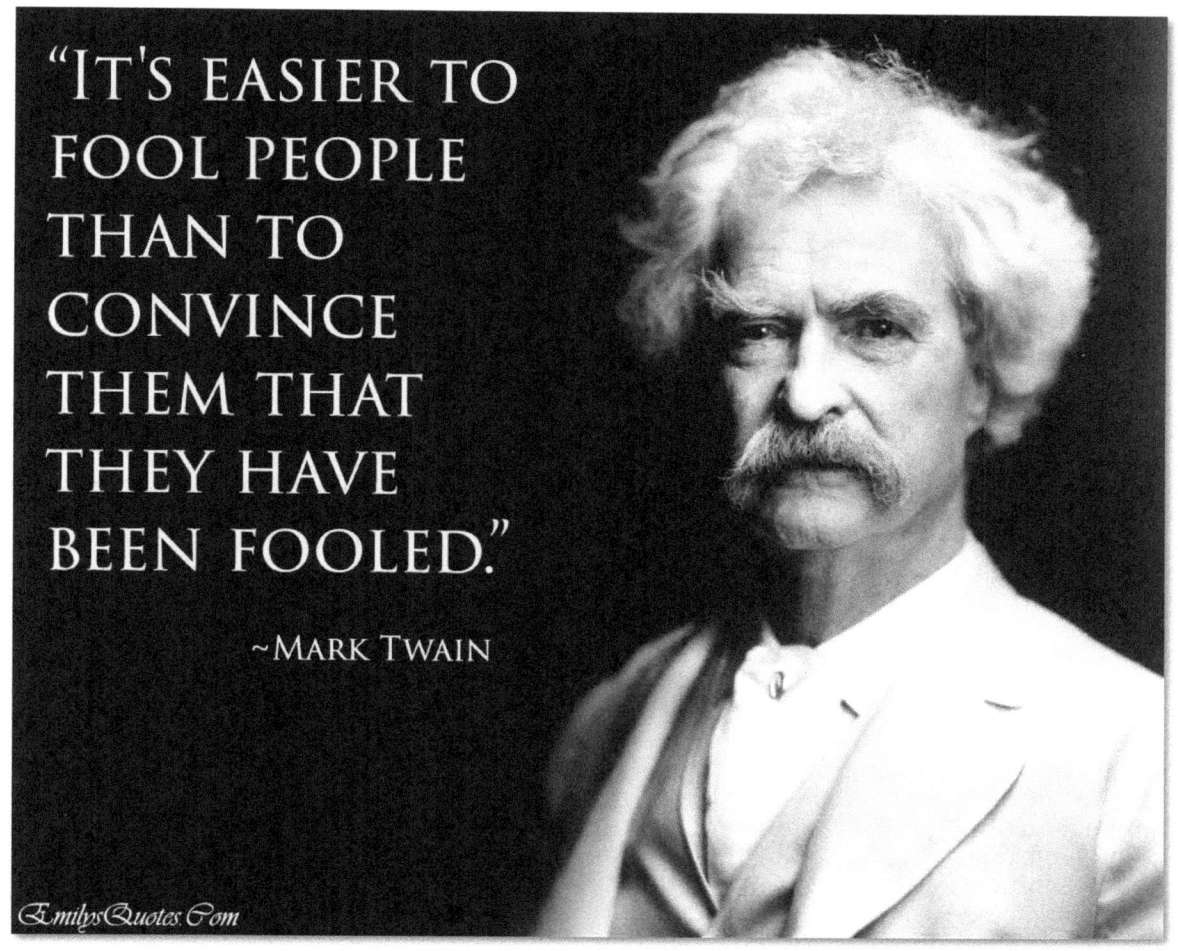

The current author was, at one time in his professional career, intimately involved with the people who engineer social consent, as Bernays referred to it, or as I have referred to the practice of this dark art "mind control." The people responsible for engineering the reader's mind to adopt self-destructive and otherwise unconscionable customs and practices were and are particularly pleased with themselves when it comes to their "pigs in a blanket" project. Members of the American public targeted for this mind control project were/are referred to by the PhD agents doing the social engineering as THE "pigs in a blanket. " The American demographic that found themselves in the crosshairs of the "pigs in a blanket" project tended to be more conservative, reactionary,[83] and laudably patriotic.

---

[83] By "reactionary" we describe a person who reacts to perceived violations of their freedom with defiance. Social engineers manipulated this laudable characteristic to yoke such sacred rights as freedom of speech and the right to bear arms with eating pigs. If the reader would just stop and process that last sentence you may, if you come to your senses, marvel at the deviousness of the

They were up against some of the brightest people on earth and, as I describe them, also the most devious. Social engineers had an unlimited budget to co-opt patriotic and freedom-loving people's attention away from the overarching plans of the people behind this social engineering project. This was done in large measure because the overarching plans of the people behind it could not care less about the people or animals targeted in this food choice social engineering project.

To pull off this social engineering legerdemain experts used a halo effect[84] operation where they took the hallowed virtues of freedom of speech and the right to bear arms, and then slipped in the eating of pigs—an animal more intelligent than a dog—then yoked them together as one in the same in the brainstem of the victim.

To the uninitiated this sounds ludicrous on its face, but it worked like a charm. Social engineers were able to conflate two incongruous things in the brainstems of their victims: 1. Eating pigs, and 2. Being a proud American patriot who believes in freedom, the right to bear arms, and beer—Beer? The working man's alcohol, i.e., beer, tells you who these social engineers targeted. The people who engineered this travesty find the eating of pigs, i.e. bacon, personally abhorrent, a fact known to their victims but disconnected from their rational mind. If the targets of this highly successful social engineering ploy were to think for just one moment, they might pause just long enough to ask—"wait a minute, this doesn't even make sense." But they can't do that, because social engineers inoculated them against anyone, including the current author, who would dare untangle their devious plot. Nevertheless, the mind control strategies and psychological operations were so clever and well funded; the result was a fait accompli. The principals who actually carried out the "pigs in a blanket" project would laugh until they cried when they recounted to one another the way their damnable (their descriptor) victims fell for their devious plot. So, if you are up in arms over my attempt to deprogram you?

---

people who mold you to defend what they want to sell you—even though these same people would never consume pigs themselves.

[84] The halo effect references the fact that some ideas, people, images carry a halo with them. By placing a person, object or idea that does not have a halo or is dark by its very nature near the halo person, object or idea, the notion is that the halo will spill over onto the dark person, object or idea. You see this in rape trials where the defendant (dark person) is seated next to and often touched by a female (halo) associate or lawyer.

Like I said, the deprogramming vaccination they slipped into their project works quite well. Let's hope next year's SARS-CoV-2 vaccination will be as equally effective.

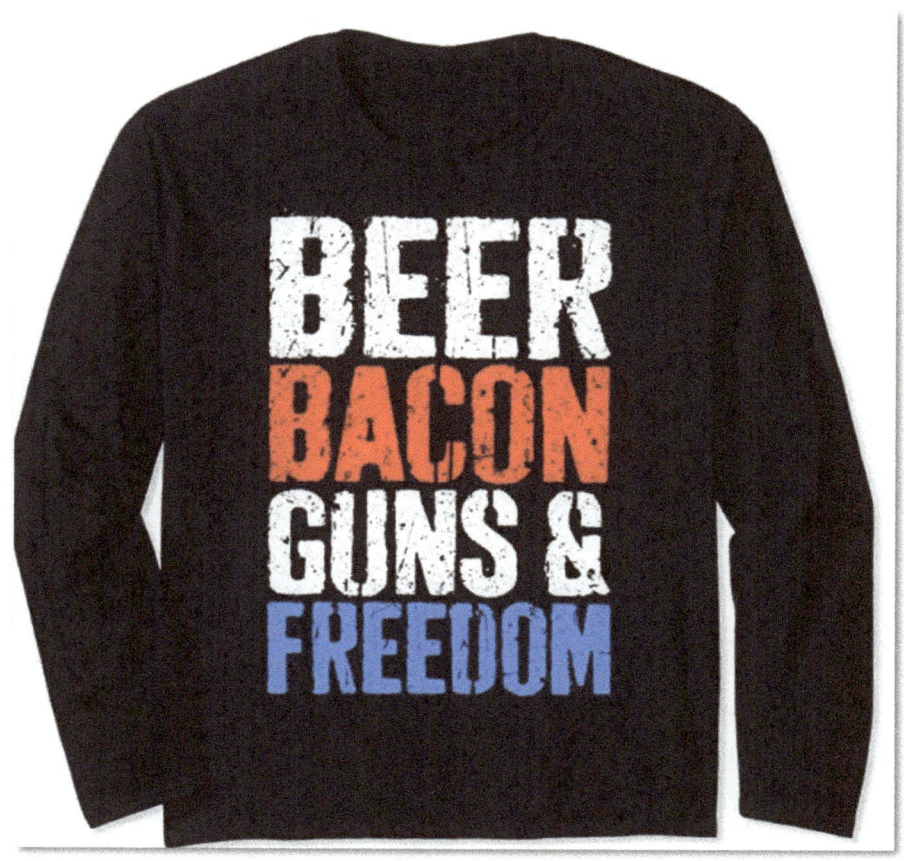

Pigs Appear Nowhere in the Declaration of Independence or the Constitution of the USA

We've already covered the horrendous mental health toll on slaugtherhouse workers who kill sentient beings for a living. Now, take a look at how COVID-19 has impacted them. First of all, the general public may be aware that nursing homes and prisons have been fertile Petri dishes for SARS-CoV-2, but did you know that industrialized kill plants have become national hot spots for SARS-CoV-2? Of the 25 largest clusters of COVID-19 cases in the United States, six are tied to meat processing plants. At least 48 slaughterhouse workers have died from the virus, and another 11,000 have been sickened—an exponentially out-of-proportion number when a per capita correction is made.

Smithfield Temporarily Shuts Pork Plant Due to Coronavirus

A Smithfield Foods pork processing plant in South Dakota will temporarily close for cleaning after more than 80 employees were confirmed to have the coronavirus, the company announced. [85]

Smithfield Slaughterhouse Specializing in the Butchering of Pigs in South Dakota

Economics and virus amplification industries of which the meat industry has no equal are dangerous bedfellows, to wit:

> "[A] new breed of meatpackers, led by Iowa Beef Packers (IBP), introduced a business model that relied on lower-cost, higher-volume production in much larger and mechanized plants with lower-skilled labor. [T]oday, two-thirds of meatpacking workers are people of color, and roughly half are immigrants." [86]

Nothing could be more American than baseball, right? Take a look at this mural of Smithfield's, that is, WH Group of China's industrial kill plant in Vernon, California.

---

[85] Associated Press, April 9, 2020.
[86] Open Markets Institute. Meatpacking More Dangerous Today Than a Generation Ago, Amplifying COVID-19 Crisis. By: Claire Kelloway in Newsletter, Resiliency, Slaughterhouse Labor.

Farmer John Mural at Smithfield's-WH Group of China's Industrial Kill Plant in Vernon, CA

A Happy Pig Wearing an L.A. Dodger's Baseball Cap

More than 100 workers at the Farmer John plant in Vernon have contracted the coronavirus in an outbreak plaguing the facility that produces the Dodger Dog.

> *"Thus far, 116 workers at the Smithfield-owned meat-processing plant have tested positive, according to the Los Angeles County Department of Public Health. Smithfield, which bought Farmer John in 2017, [87] could not be reached Saturday for comment. According to the company's website, "every employee involved in handling, preparing and processing food wears personal protective equipment covering their heads, faces (including masks and face shields), hands and bodies. Additionally, employees undergo temperature checks and are screened for COVID-19 symptoms."* [88]

The PR folks use the name "*Farmer John*" on their industrial wet kill plant in Vernon, California. A beautiful mural adorns the building where you see a peaceful pastoral scene, a sexy girl in her Daisy Dukes strolling along, a Tom Sawyer character enjoying his boyhood days. This is where they turn out the *Dodger Dogs* sold at Dodger Stadium, and it is also the place where hundreds of living animals are butchered alive every day in this wet market processing plant, in what cannot be described as anything but a virus amplification house of horrors—like ALL slaughterhouses.

> *"Hundreds of pigs are trucked each day into the facility at 3049 E. Vernon Ave., where they are killed and turned into Dodger Dogs and the ham, bacon, sausage and hot dogs sold under the Farmer John label at supermarkets and restaurants."* [89]

---

[87] Please note that the story did not mention that Smithfield is owned outright by WH Group of China.
[88] Los Angeles Times, May 24, 2020.
[89] By City News Service•Published May 23, 2020•Updated on May 24, 2020 at 11:32 am

Pigs Dying of Thirst as They Await Their Fate at Farmer John's Industrial Wet Kill Plant in Vernon, California

So Called "Downer" Being Dragged Away Because the Pig Has Collapsed out of Fear (locations unidentified for security reasons)

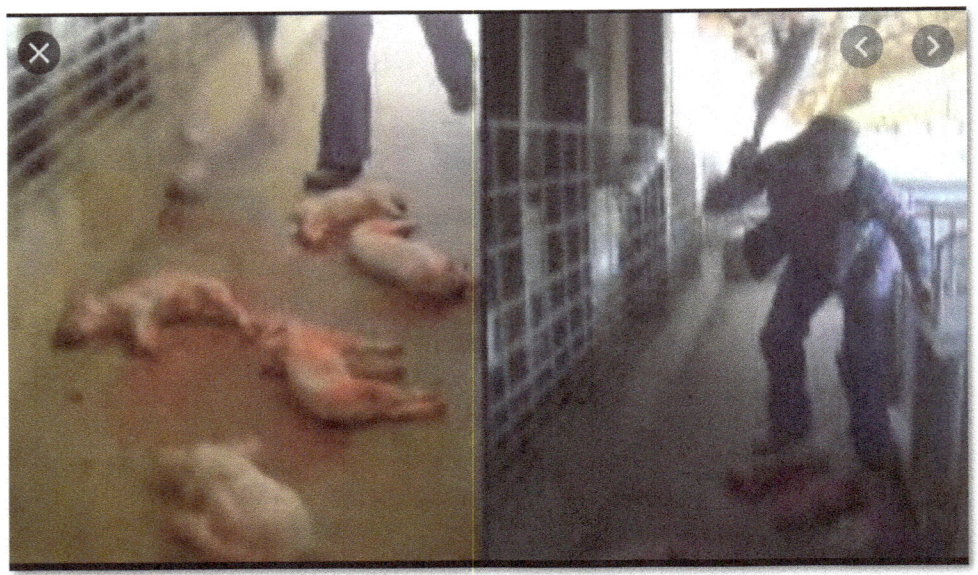

Pounding Baby Pigs onto the Killing Plant's Wet Floor, then Beaten if still Crying or Gasping for Air (locations unidentified for security reasons)

These are the "Big Four" wet market killing meat processing plants in the USA. The kill numbers listed here are under-represented, because these data are from 2011.

Cargill

- Cargill Meat Solutions Corp. Wichita, Kan.
- ***Daily slaughter capacity 29,000***
- U.S. market share 21 percent
- Beef sales: Cargill Meat Solutions would not release this data. Its parent company, Cargill Inc., reported $88.3 billion in sales in 2009.

- Company overview

    Cargill Meat Solutions is one of 75 businesses under Cargill Inc., the largest privately-held corporation in the United States. Cargill runs the biggest flour-milling company in the world, is a leading corn syrup and soybean processor, and has cocoa and chocolate operations on four continents. It employs 131,000 people in 66 countries, including Canada, Mexico and China.

JBS USA Greeley, Colo.

- JBS USA Greeley, Colo.
- ***Daily slaughter capacity 28,600***
- U.S. market share 18.5 percent
- Beef sales $9.2 billion
- Company overview

    JBS USA bought Swift (the-third largest packer) in 2007, then bought Smithfield (the fifth-largest packer and largest U.S. feedlot owner) in 2008, then bought Pilgrim's Pride, the largest chicken processor, in 2009. The company tried to buy National Beef Packing Co. in 2008, but the U.S. Department of Justice opposed the acquisition. The parent company, Brazil-based JBS S.A., is the largest beef packer in the world, with 54 processing plants on four continents.

National Beef Packing Co., LLC Kansas City, Mo.

- **Daily slaughter capacity 14,000**
- U.S. market share 10.5 percent
- Beef sales $5.4 billion
- Company overview

National Beef started as a single plant in Kansas in 1992. Its other main product is leather.

Tyson Foods Springdale, Ark.

- **Daily slaughter capacity 28,700**
- U.S. market share 25 percent
- Beef sales $12.7 billion

- Company overview

    Tyson bought the world's largest supplier of premium beef and pork products, IBP Inc., in 2001. It's the second-largest pork and chicken packer in the U.S. and sells its products in 90 countries. [90]

Experts in virology have been sounding the air raid siren for years about a deadly pandemic that is the inevitable result of a meat industry that plays Russian roulette with pathogens and their host organisms. Compare what experts in virology have been warning you about for years to what governments and the media entertainment complex and their employees have been telling you. And why would the media entertainment complex tell you anything different than the truth? Could it be economic self-interest? Let's take a look at the lobbying efforts of the meat industry for 2019:

Meat processing & products: Lobbying, 2019

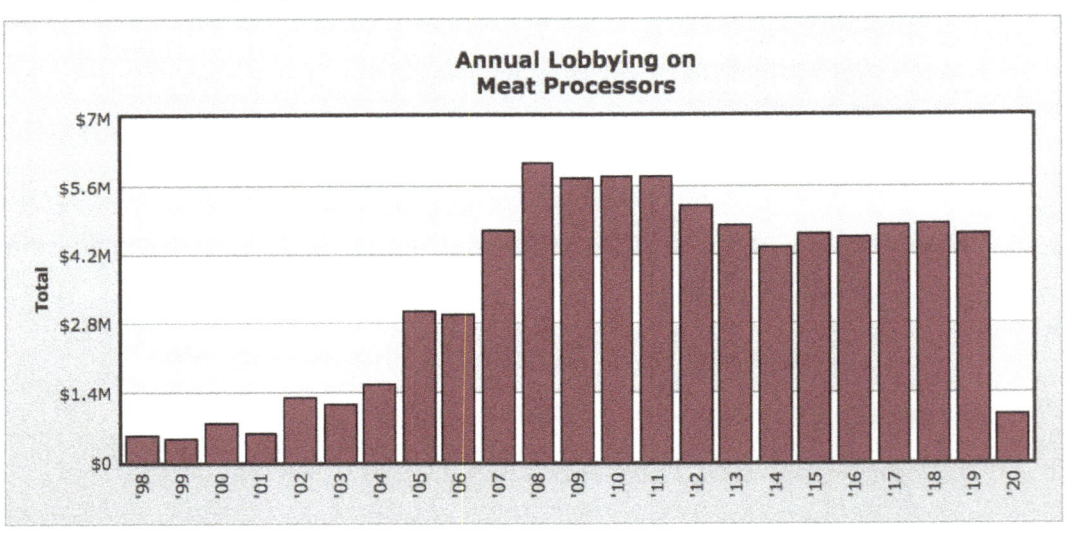

---

[90] High Country News. *The Big Four Meat Packers.* By: Emilene Ostlend, March 21, 2011.

Total for Meat processing & products: $4,587,201
Total Number of Clients Reported: 13
Total Number of Lobbyists Reported: 50
Total Number of Revolvers: 37 (74.0%)

Client	Affiliate	Total
Agri Beef	-	$80,000
Hormel Foods	-	$616,000
JBS SA	JBS USA	$498,000
Johnsonville Sausage	-	$30,000
Memphis Meats	-	$100,000
North American Meat Institute	-	$309,042
North American Renderers Assn	-	$80,000
Pacific Salmon Treaty Coalition	-	$40,000
Transhumance Holding	-	$40,000
Tyson Foods	-	$1,334,159
WH Group	Smithfield Foods	$1,460,000

[91]

Now take a look at the advertising budget for just ONE meat processor, Tyson Foods, that goes into the pockets of the media entertainment complex:

Advertising expenses of Tyson Foods worldwide 2012-2019

Published by M. Shahbandeh, Nov 15, 2019

The timeline shows the advertising expenditure of Tyson Foods worldwide from 2012 to 2019. In 2019, Tyson Foods' advertising expenses amounted to approximately 276 million U.S. dollars. Tyson Foods is a manufacturer of food products, mostly chicken, beef, and pork products.

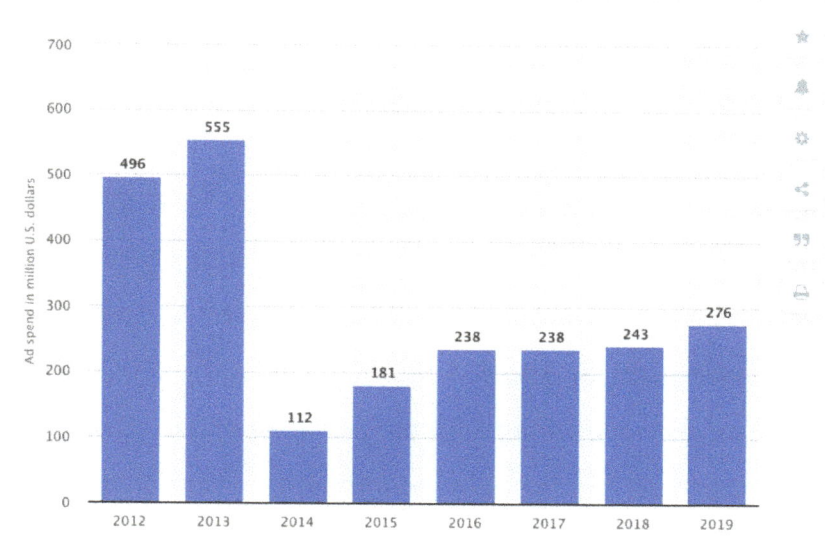

[92]

---

[91] Opensecrets.org. Meat processing & products: Lobbying, 2019.
[92] Statista: Advertising expenses of Tyson Foods worldwide 2012-2019
Published by M. Shahbandeh, Nov 15, 2019.

Beneficiaries of industries whose very business model can't help but create a never-ending series of contagious pathogens, including some very nasty SARS-type viruses, have a vested interest in a public that remains relatively ignorant about the hand-and-glove relationship between deadly viruses and what they eat. But it is not as though we have not been warned, and I am not limiting my attention to some of our greatest minds ever to have shared their thoughts on the subject, e.g., Einstein, Tesla, Newton, Franklin, Lincoln, Confucius, Leonardo, Pascal, and Voltaire, et al. The prestigious American Journal of Public Health long ago sounded the alarm on this issue *back in 2007* while we still had time to change our behaviors—we did not, to wit:

> *"As the number of human deaths from avian influenza grows and as the disease spreads geographically, fears of a 21st century influenza epidemic or pandemic mount. Even if the disease does not reach epidemic proportions imminently, the fears are nonetheless well founded. Inductive reasoning leads to the conclusion that an influenza epidemic will arise, as such epidemics have arisen many times before, including 3 times during the 20th century. The relevant questions, therefore, are when the next one will emerge and how bad it will be.* [1] *Avian influenza is just one of dozens of zoonotic diseases that have caused and will cause considerable human fear, suffering, and death. (Indeed, some have suggested that "[a]ll human viral infections were initially zoonotic in origin,"* [2(p6)] *although the precise animal source and route of transmission to humans is often a matter of some dispute.) I cannot mention all of these diseases; thus, only some well-known examples are provided, along with the probable source. There is at least some evidence that, similar to avian influenza, severe acute respiratory syndrome arose in the live-animal (i.e., "wet") markets of China.* [3] *Variant Creutzfeldt-Jakob disease probably arose from bovine spongiform encephalopathy* (BSE).[4,5] *And the source of HIV, which causes AIDS, is widely thought to be the simian immunodeficiency virus that is found in nonhuman primates.* [6,7] *Although some zoonoses are probably*

unavoidable, much human suffering resulting from zoonotic diseases could probably have been avoided had humans treated animals better. Consider, for example, the wet markets from which an influenza or severe acute respiratory syndrome epidemic may be launched. In these markets, live animals of diverse kinds are kept in large numbers and in cruelly close quarters ready for sale and fresh slaughter. The concentration of animals, their overlapping sojourns in the markets (allowing disease to spread through vast numbers of animals), and their interactions with humans (facilitating human infection) make these markets ripe for zoonoses.[8] Once an epidemic starts among animals, it can spread to animals reared in less cruel conditions. If humans did not eat wet market animals, there would be fewer of them (because fewer would be bred), the animals would not suffer from being housed in close quarters, and they would not be slaughtered. Consequently, the risk of zoonoses would be greatly diminished. In the case of variant Creutzfeldt-Jakob disease, humans would not have become infected had some humans not killed or eaten cows infected with BSE. Moreover, BSE would not spread among cattle if humans did not process the neural matter from BSE-infected cattle, to produce feed for other cattle, a practice prompted by the volume of cattle humans eat. If the plausible hypothesis that HIV resulted from simian immunodeficiency virus is indeed true, then the most likely causal route of transmission was through infected simian blood during the butchering of these animals. The butchering itself was most likely for the purposes of providing nonhuman primate meat ("bushmeat") for human consumption, a practice that continues today. It is unlikely, of course, that those who make use of animals in the above ways will recognize their treatment of animals as maltreatment. However, there is good reason for characterizing it as such. There is now an ample body of philosophical literature that compellingly demonstrates that the ways in which most humans treat animals is wrong.[9–12] Almost all humans can now not only survive but also thrive without consuming animal flesh or using animal skins and furs. Thus those who persist in these practices treat the most important animal interests—interests in continued life and the avoidance of suffering—as less important than very trivial human interests, including carnivorous gastronomic experiences.¹³ Even those who deny that there is anything wrong with treating animals in this way should now recognize that thwarting important animal interests sometimes causes considerable harm to humans, even if some minor human interests are satisfied along the way. It is curious, therefore, that changing the way humans treat animals—most basically, ceasing to eat them or, at the very least, radically limiting the quantity of them that are eaten—is largely off the radar as a significant preventive measure. **Such a change, if sufficiently adopted or imposed, could still reduce the chances of the much-feared influenza epidemic. It would be even more likely to prevent unknown future diseases that, in the absence of this change, may result from farming animals intensively and from killing them for food. Yet humanity does not consider this option.** *(Emphasis added: author's note, keep in mind Dr. Benatar penned this editorial in 2007). Insofar as the focus is not on cures for the resultant diseases, attention is only given to lesser preventive measures. Some of these, such as slaughtering animals before they are brought to markets, may bring modest improvements to the treatment of animals. However, other preventive measures, such as developing a vaccine, do not require humans to improve their treatment of animals at all. Indeed, the curative and many of the preventive measures on which humans focus are ones that often involve further suffering and death for animals. For example, because humans have contracted diseases from maltreating animals, others then experiment on animals in a bid to find either a vaccine or a cure for the diseases that result from the maltreatment. Although these medical interventions are being developed, millions of animals are culled, often* *painfully, in the hope of preventing imminent disease or epidemic in humans. Even those who think that experimenting on animals for human medical benefit is not wrong should be at least somewhat troubled by such experimentation when the ailment it seeks to fix could have been prevented. They should be even more troubled when the relevant prevention would have been to take animal interests more seriously. In response, it may be said that even if current diseases could have been prevented, they were not, and thus scientists must do what they can now to minimize human suffering and death. Whether or not one agrees with this argument, it cannot justify failing to take the preventive measures now that would obviate the need for employing them repeatedly in the future. Failure to think ahead cannot repeatedly be excused. Humanity's continued consumption of animals is not only morally problematic but also highly imprudent. Preventive action that focuses exclusively on the proximate causes of disease and plague is more risky than long-term preventive action that attends to equally crucial upstream causal factors. To rely on neutralizing a proximate cause leaves little or no room for error. The longer view, by contrast, enables one to prevent a threat before it becomes imminent. Thus, there are many more opportunities for prevention. Humans have suffered a great deal as a result of the mistreatment of animals, but that does not make the human suffering a punishment for the mistreatment; it is merely a consequence. Speaking of a causal connection does not imply an intentional agent administering the consequent as retribution for the antecedent. In any event, those humans who suffer are not just the ones responsible for animal mistreatment. Innocents are often adversely affected. When the (infected) chickens come home to roost, it may be another person, possibly from the next generation, who suffers or dies from avian influenza. Those who consume animals not only harm those animals and endanger themselves, but they also threaten the well-being of other humans who currently or will later inhabit the planet. To switch avian images, it is time for humans to remove their heads from the sand and recognize the risk to themselves that can arise from their maltreatment of other species.* [93, 94]

Back to the Future

We began this book with a review of the science behind how SARS-CoV-2 spread exponentially in some parts of the world, but not in others. We provided the reader with a substantive review of how the SARS-CoV-2 virus spreads from person to person. We took inventory of how nominal public health behavior is either a virus' best friend, or its mortal enemy—and this goes for all infectious pathogens, not just the one responsible for COVID-19. And if you haven't figured it out by now, let me state it explicitly. The draconian edicts from public officials that so many oppose would have never been necessary, and certainly not so easily justifiable, were it not for the American publics' virus-friendly public health behavior; most notably, their food choices. That means the general public has more control over

---

[93] September 2007, Vol 97, No. 9, American Journal of Public Health.
[94] References for American Journal of Public Health Article
1. Osterholm MT. Preparing for the next pandemic. New England Journal of Medicine. 2005; 352:1839–1842.
2. Weber J, Alcorn K. Origins of HIV and the AIDS epidemic. MedGenMed. 2000;2(4):1–6.
3. Guan Y, Zheng BJ, He YQ, et al. Isolation and characterization of viruses related to the SARS coronavirus from animals in Southern China. Science. 2003;302:276–278.
4. Will RG, Ironside JW, Zeidler M, et al. A new variant of Creutzfeldt-Jakob disease in the UK. Lancet. 1996; 347: 921–925.
5. Scott MR, Will RG, Ironside J, et al. Compelling transgenic evidence for transmission of bovine spongiform en- cephalopathy prions to humans. Proc Natl Acad Sci USA. 1999;96: 15137–15142.
6. Gao F, Bailes E, Robertson DL, et al. Origin of HIV-1 in the chimpanzee Pan troglodytes troglodytes. Nature. 1999; 397:436–441.
7. Sharp P, Bailes E, Chaudhuri RP, Rodenburg CM, Santiago MO, Hahn BH. The origins of acquired immune deficiency syndrome viruses: where and when? Philos Trans R Soc Lond B Biol Sci. 2001; 356:867–876.
8. Webster RG. Wet markets—a continuing source of severe acute respiratory syndrome and influenza? Lancet. 2004;365:234–236.
9. Singer P. Animal Liberation. 2nd ed.
New York, NY: Random House Trade; 1990.
10. Reagan T. The Case for Animal Rights. Berkeley: University of California Press; 1983.
11. DeGrazia D. Taking Animals Seriously. Cambridge, England: Cambridge University Press; 1996.
12. Rowlands M. Animals Like Us. London, England: Verso; 2002.
13. Benatar D. Duty and the beast: animal experimentation and neglected interests. QJM. 2000; 93:831–835.

this current pandemic, and the one waiting in the wings, than they realize if they could psychologically inoculate themselves against the 24/7 behavioral modeling to which they are subjected, some of which has been covered here. If the reader is interested in behavioral modeling and how it works in detail, we suggest this book. [95] Here is a brief excerpt from the aforementioned book regarding how you were conditioned to eat what your controllers wanted you to eat:

"Bernays was hired by pork producers to manipulate the public's view of "heavy" breakfasts, e.g., bacon and eggs. In the 1920s and before Bernays socially engineered breakfast behavior, the average American breakfast consisted of toast, coffee or tea. Bernays concocted a manipulative survey and sent it to a group of physicians as the first step in his devious PSYOP. Bernays understood that when it comes to any survey, the nature of the question and how it is asked virtually guarantees the nature of the answer.

For instance, if you want to dupe the public into supporting a high-speed rail boondoggle, you ask this question: Wouldn't it be wonderful if you could travel from San Diego to San Francisco in an hour and a half on a luxury bullet train? The vast majority of people will say yes to that question. But if you inquire of voters about how they may feel about a high speed bullet train using objective questions, you get the exact opposite response, e.g. "Are you willing to have your taxes raised to build a high speed rail system that will service a limited number of business travelers who want to go from San Diego to San Francisco on a train in roughly the same time and cost it takes to fly there now?

Bernays framed his survey to physicians this way, and I paraphrase: "Which is better, no breakfast or a breakfast consisting of bacon and eggs?" Once Bernays got the responses he knew he would get, he sent the results to another group of 5,000 physicians. He

---

[95] Shadow Men (2015), An Encyclopedia of Mind Control. Anthony Napoleon, PhD, VBW Publishing, College Station, Texas.

simultaneously sent out a press release. (Once again, to the dupes in the press) It wasn't long before bacon and eggs became THE stereotypical mainstay breakfast in America. After all, the herd instinct had been triggered with advice from doctors, that is, doctors who had been manipulated by the nephew of one of the greatest psychoanalysts of all time." [96]

At one time in America, responsible hygienic public health behavior was routinely taught in public schools. It was part of the curricula. Moreover, at one time in America, teaching manners—aka, being considerate of other people—was job number one for parents. In the late 1950s, a film was produced for an audience comprised of public grammar school children. In part it was produced as a response to the avian flu of that era. The film was entitled "Mr. Bungle." The film taught responsible public health values. It gently shamed selfish, brutish, garish, and otherwise inconsiderate children. Here are a few things the film highlighted:

- Covering one's mouth when coughing or sneezing
- Hand washing after going to the restroom
- Having in your possession a handkerchief or tissue
- Lunchroom manners that gently shamed selfish and inconsiderate behavior
- Why it is wrong to go through life advocating solely for your own interests without being considerate of others, including keeping your germs to yourself.

The writers of the film avoided script lines that would ridicule the young actor who was depicted in the film engaging in virus-friendly, rude, and selfish behaviors. Behaviors, I might add, that everyone reading this hates when they are subjected to them. Each time the boy engaged in one of these virus-friendly, selfish behaviors, he was reminded that he should reconsider his selfish behavior because he didn't want to become a "Mr. Bungle." The term "bungle" comes from the word "bungler," as in: "failing do something properly, failing at a task, job." In the film, the job or task was

---

[96] Napoleon, Anthony. (2015) Shadow Men: An Encyclopedia of Mind Control. VBW Publishing, College Station, Texas. Edward Bernays was the nephew of Sigmund Freud.

to be socially responsible. It was your job to NOT spread your germs. Your job was to be considerate and thoughtful of others.

The boy who starred in the film, and the character he played, had something that would soon be erased in subsequent generations; i.e., a conscience. It was his sense of conscience that made teaching him possible. Remarkably, subsequent generations of Americans used this film as fodder to fuel their hysterical guffaws (LOL, ROFL, etc.) at anything that would dare bridle their self-aggrandizement and self-focus. After all, these people were told during their formative years that they were the center of the universe. In fact, trendy ideologues have glibly referred to this film that taught people to cover their mouths when they coughed or sneezed, and to be respectful of others, as "propaganda."

Mr Bungle 1950's propaganda School film

Since the COVID-19 pandemic, I ask the guffawing critics of the film who referred to it as "propaganda" this question: Who's laughing now?

It is easy to forget that **before** COVID-19, America's nominal pathogen-friendly public health behavior was directly responsible for billions of dollars of health care costs, untold personal misery, and insults to your pocketbook. To express that thought another way, COVID-19 added insult to a preexisting injury.

"The estimated average annual total economic burden of influenza to the healthcare system and society was $11.2 billion ($6.3–$25.3 billion).

> *Direct medical costs were estimated to be $3.2 billion ($1.5–$11.7 billion) and indirect costs $8.0 billion ($4.8–$13.6 billion). These total costs were based on the estimated average numbers of (1) ill-non medically attended patients (21.6 million), (2) office-based outpatient visits (3.7 million), (3) emergency department visits (0.65 million) (4) hospitalizations (247.0 thousand), (5) deaths (36.3 thousand) and (6) days of productivity lost (20.1 million)."[97]*

Each year, individual American households spend over $300 on cold and flu type medicines.

> *The average consumer shops for over-the-counter medicine 26 times each year. That's $338 per household, according to data collected by the Consumer Healthcare Products Association.* [98]

The term "common cold" is another case study in how the American public causes itself untold misery because of how their nominal public health behavior is pathogen-friendly and inconsiderate. The name "common cold" suggests "no big deal," but it is a big deal. Our own studies have shown that when a person is feeling well, they fall for the innocuous name of the malady Rhinoviruses cause, but when they find themselves in the throes of a sore throat, body aches, and no appetite, they think differently about it. And in particular, they often have a person in mind who gave them the virus—and they are not happy with that person(s). The cost of the "common cold" alone is staggering and is totally unnecessary, if only people developed a better understanding of how viruses are transmitted, and then took that information and showed some common decency to others. As you review the economic costs of the common cold, ask yourself whether the mind modelers who have created a cultural norm that encourages people to "suck it up" when it comes to cold and flu misery had your best interests in mind—or theirs?

---

[97] Wayan C.W.S. Putri, David J. Muscatello, Melissa S. Stockwell, Anthony T. Newall. (2018) *Economic burden of seasonal influenza in the United States.* https://doi.org/10.1016/j.vaccine.2018.05.057

[98] Department of Health and Human Services. Observations on Trends in Prescription Drug Spending March 8, 2016.

> *"The common cold costs the United States up to $40 billion per year (as of 2001) and upwards of $75 million (as of 2018). Even using 2001 data, indirect costs due to lost productivity from absences at work make up the majority: $22.5 billion. Direct costs include $7.7 billion for physician visits and $2.9 billion for over-the-counter drugs. The figure also includes $1.1 billion per year on an estimated 41 million antibiotic prescriptions, even though antibiotics have no effect on colds and contributing to antibiotic resistance is a considerable concern."* [99]

Many Americans scoff at merely asking the following questions: Do you know how many people you hurt when you go to work sick? Do you know how much it costs your employer? Here are some numbers from 2018 that might get your attention, even if you are one of those people who found "Mr. Bungle" to be propaganda. Here is the headline from the following analysis:

THE $9 BILLION REASON YOU SHOULD NEVER SHOW UP TO WORK SICK

> *"[O]utplacement consulting firm Challenger, Gray & Christmas, Inc. estimates that the flu **costs employers more than $9.4 billion in lost productivity**."* [100]

How our culture found itself in this dismal place has been the subject of the current author's attention for years, with causes and cures explicated in some of his other writings. [101]

Summary

The COVID-19 pandemic has provided the American public, along with their kindred spirits everywhere in the developed world, a golden opportunity to reexamine what should constitute nominal public health behaviors. Here are some

---

[99] MDLinx. Will scientists cure the common cold? By: John Murphy, October 15, 2018.
[100] Business Insider. The $9 billion reason you should never show up to work sick. By: Rachel Gillett. January 19, 2018.
[101] Napoleon, Anthony (2012), The Progressive Virus. VBW Publishing, College Station, Texas.

suggestions, none of which will encroach on Constitutionally protected freedoms, shutter businesses, or do anything except make public spaces safer for everyone. If these behaviors become nominal in American culture, I can virtually guarantee that the reader and your loved ones will be spared countless days, weeks and months feeling miserable due to any number of infectious diseases. And, in the case of serious pathogens like SARS-CoV-2, these behaviors may save your life or the life of a loved one. I can virtually guarantee that America's economy will never have to be shuttered again when the next rogue virus makes its appearance (and it will) in our country if these simple—dare I say common sense—recommendations are followed. Isn't that what responsible behavior is all about—making things better for you, your loved ones, our country, and the rest of the world?

1. If you are sick, stay at home at least for the first few days when you are most likely to be at your most infectious.

2. Businesses and employees should not be financially punished when sick people stay at home. Politicians need to take action now.

3. People who feel under the weather should wear face protection and wash their hands frequently, just like people in many other parts of the world.

4. Automatic temperature scans should be made before being allowed to enter a gym, restaurant, amusement park, aircraft, or other public conveyances or crowded public venues where people will come into close contact with one another.[102] If you have a temperature of 100 F/38C, you should be asked to go home and take care of yourself and/or see your doctor.[103]

5. Businesses must be strongly encouraged to provide cleansing stations before entering, for example, a buffet area.[104]

---

[102] We understand that some pathogens, like SARS-CoV-2 for example, do not cause a fever during the first part of its infection profile. That said, 90 percent of contagious pathogens do cause a fever.
[103] The average normal body temperature is generally accepted as 98.6°F (37°C). Some studies have shown that the "normal" body temperature can have a wide range, from 97°F (36.1°C) to 99°F (37.2°C). A temperature over 100.4°F (38°C) most often means you have a fever caused by an infection or illness.
[104] Disney Cruise Lines have set up beautiful hand washing stations where patrons entering one of the dining areas must wash their hands before entering. Disney has managed to protect its guests from not only respiratory viruses, but also the G.I. pathogens that have plagued so many other cruise lines over the years.

6. People should voluntarily bring along a "cough or sneeze" cloth when going out in public made of antiviral material and/or embedded with antimicrobials.

7. Businesses should routinely and politely ask patrons who repeatedly cough or sneeze to go home and get well.

8. It should become the norm that when people engage in irresponsible public health behavior, that other people say something polite and considerate to that person, along the lines of, "If you are sick, you probably shouldn't spread your germs." Others must learn to join in and stop becoming the person who stands by silently while their more socially responsible fellow citizens do all the work. You don't have to be rude, and it won't be necessary if everyone does the right thing and speaks up.

Epilogue

Editor's note: The author provided a draft of this manuscript for review and invited questions. What follows are some of the questions asked of the author, along with his answers.

You seem to be really interested in viruses, how did that come about?

Dr. Napoleon: When I was 15 years old I attended a lecture on viruses. The professor posed the question "are viruses living?" That question motivated me to write my first paper on viruses. I recall the paper examined the Bacteriophage virus. During my clinical training years later in medical psychology, the AIDS crisis hit, and I happened to be a chief intern on an inpatient hospital ward at a large city hospital that treated dual diagnosis patients, i.e., mental illness and substance abuse, with many of our patients using IV-routed drugs where infectious diseases are commonplace. None of us at the time knew very much about this new infection, including how contagious it might be, because of how new it was. One of my supervisors, who also happened to be a neurosurgeon, was an expert on viruses. I think because of that, he demanded that all the interns wash our hands dozens of times a day with chlorhexidine. I recall once sitting down on the edge of a patient's bed, and he saw me do this and he pulled me aside to warn me about contact transmission of viruses and how long they remain viable on various and sundry surfaces. Later I worked in a plastic surgery practice as a medical psychologist fellow, where the chief surgeon boasted that none of his patients had ever developed a post-op infection secondary to the surgery. This was because all of the doctors, nurses, and support staff were held to super-high standards of hygiene. Later in my life, I became a consultant to people who were interested in germ warfare and some of the strategic issues involved in that subject. Becoming knowledgeable about viruses goes with that territory.

You wrote that in November of 2019 you had your staff begin wearing respirator facemasks? Is that right? And if so, why did you do that?

Dr. Napoleon. Yes. I had become aware that this peculiarly infectious and virulent novel SARS-CoV was active in China sometime in the middle of November of 2019. I knew what that meant based upon my education, training, and forensic background. I hasten to add that early in November, the only thing anyone knew was that this SARS-like clinical presentation was particularly virulent. I might say I began ramping up my warnings about hand washing, respirators, and social distancing on my now-abandoned social media account with a specific admonition for people to begin wearing respirators at that time. During the time I was active on social media, I published scores of warnings and advisories on droplet infections, contagion dynamics, and how people should prepare for the next inevitable pandemic. Just as an aside, whenever I shared my expertise on these matters, it never failed: shadow banning, trolling, etc. would ramp up. My frustration over the general public's disheartening practice of waiting to protect themselves until the proverbial boot was on their throat is clearly seen in this tweet.

I have a technical question if you don't mind. Where did the SARS-CoV-2 come from or originate?

Dr. Napoleon: Perhaps the best way to answer your question is to indulge me as I think out loud about how these viruses work, and in so doing maybe we can arrive at an answer together. I'll backtrack later and add in references for you. Since you are a physician, you know that Coronaviruses (CoVs) are relatively large RNA viruses that have been traditionally associated with mild respiratory infections in humans, for example the Human CoVs of HCoVs, HCoV-229E and HCoV-OC43. Their genome's large size and the instability of some CoV replicase gene sequences means that CoVs are prone to mutate and continually remake themselves every time they commandeer the replication machinery of their host. Because of industrialized meat breeding, raising and slaughtering, and the fact that CoVs are huge and unstable replicators, we started seeing these more virulent CoVs appear one right after the other over the past 100 years. For example, the so-called SARS-CoVs like HCoV-HKU1, associated with chronic pulmonary disease (Woo et al., 2005); HCoV-NL63 that causes upper and lower respiratory tract disease in children and adults worldwide (Van der Hoek et al., 2004); and then Middle East respiratory syndrome CoV (MERS-CoV); and now SARS-CoV-2. But before SARS-CoV-2, virologists began a big push to reverse-engineer, and then reconstruct these more virulent pathogens in order to find treatments and unlock their mysteries. There was nothing malevolent about that push. After all, that is how we develop vaccines and treatments, right? So in 2006, Almazan and his team solved this reverse-engineering problem when they developed this thing called BAC, which is "bacterial artificial chromosomes." (Almazan F., Gonzalez J.M., Penzes Z., Izeta A., Calvo E., Plana-Duran J., Enjuanes L Engineering the largest RNA virus genome as an infectious bacterial artificial chromosome. Proc. Natl. Acad. Sci. U.S.A. 2000;97:5516-5521) The first lab-created SARS-CoV virus took place in 2006. By the way, that did not take place in China. Ever since 2006, virologists in sophisticated labs all over the world have been busy tinkering with these SARS-CoVs—and on an unintended but inevitable parallel tract, one much more prolific than all the virology labs in existent, the SARS-CoVs were hot-housed in the meat industry. Permit me to quote directly from Dr. Almazan's work from his groundbreaking paper regarding BAC:

> "In addition to SARS-CoV and TGEV, the BAC approach has been successfully used to engineer infectious clones of HCoV-OC43 (St-Jean et al., 2006), feline infectious peritonitis virus (FIPV) (Balint et al., 2012), and the recently emerged MERS-CoV (Almazan et al., 2013). In the last case, a combination of synthetic biology and the use of BACs allowed the generation of a MERS-CoV infectious clone only four months after the first MERS-CoV outbreak, illustrating the power of the BAC approach. Recently, modified BAC approaches have been used to generate full-length cDNA clones of the SARS-CoV strains Frankfurt-1 (Pfefferle et al., 2009) and TOR2 related clinical isolate CV7 (Tylor et al., 2009), assembled in a BAC under the control of the T7 RNA polymerase promoter. In the case of the Frankfurt-1 strain, infectious virus was rescued after transfection of the full-length transcripts derived from the in vitro transcription of the linearized BAC construct. This approach combines plasmid-based handling of the infectious clone with direct delivery of genome-like RNA into the cytoplasm, circumventing transcription of the infectious clone in the nucleus driven by the CMV promoter, and avoiding the possibility of splicing. However, although some splicing could occur during the nuclear expression of the viral genome, the efficiency of this phenomenon is very low and does not affect the recovery of infectious virus (Almazan et al., 2000). In contrast, in the case of the CV7 isolate, infectious virus was recovered in situ from cells transfected with the BAC clone and infected with a modified vaccine Ankara expressing T7 RNA polymerase. In this system an in vitro transcription step is also avoided."

Using BAC, the MERS CoV was duplicated in only four months after the MERS outbreak. Think about that: it took only 16 weeks to create a duplicate pathogen. Labs from all over the world have been creating lab-sourced SARS-CoVs for at least the last 20 years that I know of, perhaps longer.

Virologists from all over the world have been focused, I'd say for the last 10 years if not longer, on Angiotensin-converting enzyme 2's (ACE-2) proteins as receptors for the SARS-CoV-2 "S" proteins. Bats harbor SARS-CoVs without ever getting sick; in other words, they can safely harbor SARS-CoVs, so researchers were naturally interested in bats because of this. I know the lay public has never had it explained to them as to why all this interest in bats and Coronaviruses. We know that not all bats are equally susceptible to SARS-CoVs because of differences in their own ACE-2 receptors. Structural modeling of ACE-2 receptors in bats by tinkering with various amino acids, which modified their susceptibility to the "S" proteins on the SARS-CoVs, has been taking place since 2010, maybe earlier. This work was done at Wuhan Institute of Virology led by Dr. Hou, which included Dr. Shi Zhengli. They transparently published their work in 2010. Not exactly the kind of thing you'd do if you were involved in bioweapons research or up to no good.

Dr. Zhengli went on to document in 2013 that bats were the source of SARS-CoVs, using assay proof as opposed to phylogenetic evidence. But I think, specific to your question, this bat SARS-like CoV labeled WIV1 (Bat SL-CoV-WIV1), aka SARS-like CoV WIV1, found in Chinese Rufous Horseshoe bats (Rhinolophus sinicus) was discovered to be able to unlock human ACE-2 receptors without the need for an intermediate host animal. So back in 2013, they had the virus CoV WIV1 that possessed a NATURALLY occurring "S" protein that could attach to human ACE-2 receptors. But the WIV1 is not SARS-CoV-2. This technology was shared with every other virologist in the world—not exactly a secret. Kind of like, for our lay readers, open source computer code.

An event that garnered a lot of attention occurred in 2015 when researchers took the scaffolding of SARS-CoV and replaced the "S" protein that naturally occurs with the "S" protein found in the Rufous bat. This replacement "S" protein had the ability to attach to human ACE-2 proteins. For our lay readers, they may think of "scaffolding" as a generic auto body frame, which serves as the foundation upon which various models are produced. By the way, all of these genomic sequences were deposited into GenBank, [105] including the lab-created "S" protein amino acid structure. In 2015 we possessed a bioengineered SARS-CoV with an engineered "S" protein that can directly infect humans by attaching to their ACE-2 receptors. **I repeat, all of these creations were all deposited in GenBank located in the USA.** [106] I will make note of the fact that this "new" engineered SARS-CoV caused severe disease in mice, but that is what ALL SARS-CoVs do, after all; that is why they are labeled severe acute respiratory syndrome (SARS) CoVs.

So let me be very Socratic in my answer to your question, which may be the question of the day, given the COVID-19 pandemic:

- Could SARS-CoV-2 have been engineered, in whole or in part, in any number of labs, including the WIV, based upon existent SARS viruses and current technology? Yes.
- Could the SARS-CoV-2 have spontaneously occurred in the wild? Yes.
- Could the SARS-CoV-2 have come from the meat industries' unavoidable practice of amping up SARS-CoV virus replication? Yes.

We know that labs have many, many safeguards—but as I chronicled in this book, those are far from foolproof. The proximity of the WIV and patient zero gave me pause. Dr. Shi Zhengli said something in the very early part of 2020 that I found to be fascinating when she asked the following impromptu rhetorical question: *"Could **they** have come from our lab?"*[107]

---

[105] The GenBank sequence database is an open access, annotated collection of all publicly available nucleotide sequences and their protein translations. It is produced and maintained by the National Center for Biotechnology Information (NCBI; a part of the National Institutes of Health in the United States) as part of the International Nucleotide Sequence Database Collaboration (INSDC).
[106] Ibid.
[107] Scientific American. How China's 'Bat Woman' Hunted Down Viruses from SARS to the New Coronavirus. By: By Jane Qiu on April 27, 2020.

When Dr. Zhengli asked this question, I think she disclosed more than she realized at the time. Dr. Zhengli's use of the plural, when she knew that the pathogen responsible for the SARS infecting the community was a ***single CoV***, suggests that she was concerned, or at least did not rule out, that some of her engineered nucleotide sequences had escaped her lab, or that her lab had engineered more than one highly contagious and virulent SARS-CoV, and that any one of *them* could be responsible for the refractory clinical presentations reported by critical care doctors that we now recognize as SARS-CoV-2. I think she was concerned that critical building blocks of SARS-CoV-2, perhaps the sequences having to do with those unique bat "S" protein sequences that could unlock human ACE-2 receptors, had somehow made it into the community. Virologists are, by nature, perfectionists in everything they do, including their use of words. So, Dr. Zhengli's use of the plural "they" and not "it," I think, may be a tell that at the very least significant parts of the SARS-CoV-2 genome existed in her lab, probably including naturally occurring and genetically engineered sequences, and perhaps the exact 29,881 nucleotide sequence that is the blueprint for SARS-CoV-2. I could probably say the same for any number of sophisticated labs all over the world. In case you are wondering, Dr. Zhengli's English is impeccable and probably better than most of the students we have had the pleasure of teaching over the years.

Did WIV or a dozen other labs across the globe possess most, if not all, of the genetic sequences of SARS-CoV-2? Yes, of course. Do I think SARS-CoV-2 came from WIV? I don't think so in whole. Perhaps strands of its RNA structure, but probably not the entire 29,881 nucleotide sequence, and even that, I think, is unlikely; but I cannot rule it out. I honestly do not think the answer to your question is knowable, and certainly not provable in a criminal court of law, because of problems with chain of custody and the ever-changing nature of tracking down the virus in question.

Has the public's response to COVID-19 surprised you?

Dr. Napoleon: I wouldn't use the descriptor "surprise," but I certainly would say I have been disappointed and extremely compassionate at the same time. I had an older psychoanalyst professor, Viennese accent and all, during my grad years, and he would continually stress to those of us in training that this thing called civility and rationality is a paper-thin veneer that holds back stark irrationality, panic and mob behavior. COVID-19 has terrified people, and when they are terrified, they tend to regress to their primordial resting place. And I have to tell you, when people regress to primordial states of mind, the last thing they should do is "get on" social media. People game anything—that is, they take the measure of any event, good or bad, and then make virtue-less assessments of how they can benefit. On the other hand, I do see confirmation of the old saw, "When the going gets tough, the tough get going." Such people have always been in the minority, however. Once my staff knew I was writing this book, they sent to me tweets, FB posts, YouTube videos and various other media that made my heart ache. Even people who I thought were pretty rational have gone off the deep end. This is what people do when they are terrified and feel as though they have no control over a bad situation. I repeat, it is not a coincidence that every fragile theory and belief espoused by those who have been reacquainted with their primordial resting place just happen to have one thing in common. All of their beliefs and theories about COVID-19 make them feel better in a weird sort of way, because they mitigate the seriousness of this 'killer virus' itself. When I drill down on this widespread mental distress, I find the following common denominators:

- Feelings of loss of control
- Mistrust of public officials
- A dangerous reliance upon social media personalities who exploit their fears
- Financial anxiety

Taken together and over time, the sufferer spirals into a depressive state. It is my hope that by reading this book, those suffering right now can retake some control over this situation. Their mistrust of public officials and media personalities, I hope, can become more discriminative, so that not all of them are lumped into one basket. I also recommend unplugging or at the very least reducing one's time in an online community that has proven to be dangerous to your health. Helping others is a very potent elixir when you are not feeling well.

Do you think politicians or others are trying to purposefully hurt the U.S. economy by shutting it down?

Dr. Napoleon: I can assure you there are people, groups, and other vested interests I am personally familiar with who would like nothing better than exactly that. These groups are always on the lookout for ways to exploit an event for their own or their benefactor's short- and long-term aspirations. But there is a distinction that few people make, and it is this: Just because certain vested interests may try to benefit from the negative economic consequences secondary to imposed public health guidelines—going so far as to encourage governmental edicts that would cripple the economy—is not the sine qua non of those guidelines or behaviors being unnecessary or overkill, or that they were created to solely wreak havoc on America's or the world's economies, and they are certainly not proof that the COVID-19 pandemic is not real or as serious as virologists and infectious disease experts say it is.

Are we going to get through this pandemic?

Dr. Napoleon: Of course we will, and I don't want you to be so concerned because you have a lot of control over not only this germ, but others as well. We've been through these things before, and those of us who took care were most likely to come out of it even stronger. Will people be changed? Yes, our culture is changing. I suspect that working from home is going to become much more popular. Technology that allows remote interaction, especially video conferencing software and technology, are going to see boom times. I think the days of the people who cough and sneeze in public without so much as covering their mouths are no longer going to spread their germs without reprisal. The guy in the gym who coughs every two minutes is, I hope, no longer going to be tolerated by management, and the other patrons subjected to his selfish and ignorant belief that he can "work out his flu bug." I also think the politicians, media presenters, and social media mouths who have jumped on this or that bandwagon will not be soon forgotten when this thing is over, and it will end—not soon, because SARS-CoV pandemics come in waves—but it will end, and if you keep your wits about you and increase your discernment, you will be just fine.

I think those authoritarian-control obsessed politicians, bureaucrats and appointees at all levels of government became easier to spot because of the COVID-19 pandemic. Just like when Luminol is sprayed on otherwise invisible blood spatter, these authoritarian controllers light up like a Christmas tree. While their knowledge of infectious diseases is on par with a cranberry's knowledge of quantum physics, they are orgasmic over the fact that the COVID-19 pandemic was a godsend, because they had found a way to rationalize their control of their fellow human by equating behavioral shackles with saving lives. That is what they always do. Keep in mind that this genre of person could not care less about their fellow human's health or safety; they never do. It is all about control. It was impossible for them to hide their joy over their newest and best-yet excuse to exercise control over their fellow human. These controllers' insatiable need to stand before the cameras was so exciting to them that they could not, despite their best bathroom mirror-practiced caring faces, hide their orgasmic joy over imposing forced restrictions—their performances are like the SARS-CoV-2 infected person who coughs in her own face, and then takes a deep breath. Whatever power they had, whoever put up with them in the past because it was the path of least resistance, I think—I hope—those days are over. Had these people not suffered from a pathological need and joy to regulate everything, perhaps the public would have never resisted their demands. I am hopeful that our younger people want to do the right thing when it comes to their food choices. Doing the right thing is also the smart thing, and for that I am very optimistic about the future.

I leave you with these thoughts that people a hundred years from now will take for granted. Being ahead of your time is lonely, but it sure makes you look smart in the future. In 2016, the World Congress of Virology met in San Antonio, Texas. This study captured the tone of the conference and mirrors the warnings of experts like Dr. Shi Zhengli, and so many other experts in virology.

Journal of Antivirals & Antiretrovirals
Open Access

Vegetarian diet and their effect on viral diseases

8th World Congress on Virology

November 28-30, 2016 San Antonio, USA

Rashmi Sharma

Samrat Prithviraj Chouhan Government College Ajmer, India

Posters & Accepted Abstracts: J Antivir Antiretrovir

Abstract :

Vegetarian diet and their effect on human beings have been studied worldwide. There are evidences that vegetarians have lower rates of coronary heart diseases because of low LDL cholesterol, lower prevalence of obesity, lower rates of hypertension and diabetes mellitus. Cancer rates of vegetarians are lower and life expectancy is greater. The risk of colorectal cancer is lower in vegetarians .There are different categories of vegetarians. Vegans who eat no animal products Lacto-ovo-vegetarians who eat no meat but eggs and dairy foods or both Pesco-vegetarians who eat fish but other meats less than 1 time Semi-vegetarians who eat meat aside from fish occasionally but less than weekly non-vegetarians who eat meats aside from fish more than 1 time per week. Since Rajasthan tops the list of states with highest vegetarians (more than 98% population) in India, while Telangana has highest proportions of meat eaters in India. The persons fall in Lacto-vo-vegetarian group; vegetarian diet includes wheat, rice, vegetables, buckwheat, Amaranthus and fruits. Buckwheat (Fagopyrum esculentum) (family: Polygonaceae) is healthiest food and is rich in essential amino acids, manganese, magnesium, cupper, fiber, phosphorus and protein. Vegetarians have low rates of viral diseases. Vegetarians have less HPV (Human Papilloma Virus).

Were it not for the association between eating an anti-viral and compassionate diet with divisive political beliefs, unrelated to smart and compassionate dietary choices often voiced by people who tend to alienate others, those of us who have made our scientific case and who have helped to educate the public about how they came to eat what they are fed and like it and defend it as if it were a religion, not a food choice, would have persuaded many more people to do the right thing and be smart at the same time. If we had done that, we'd be a much healthier country, and events like COVID-19 would most likely have never occurred—or if it did, it would have been a mere shadow of its current self. Until that time, how many more pandemics will it take before the pathogen vectors that walk among us come to their senses or virtue is imposed upon them?

> "I WAS BOLD IN THE PURSUIT OF KNOWLEDGE, NEVER FEARING TO FOLLOW TRUTH AND REASON TO WHATEVER RESULTS THEY LED." - THOMAS JEFFERSON
>
> *Inspirationfeed.com*

Karma has no menu. You get served what you deserve.

"Vegetarianism is a greater progress. From the greater clearness of head and quicker apprehension motivated him to become a vegetarian. Flesh-eating is an unprovoked murder."

- Benjamin Franklin

"That we can subsist on plant food and perform our work even to advantage is not a theory but a well-demonstrated fact. Many races living almost exclusively on vegetables are of superior physique and strength. Every effort should be made to stop the wanton, cruel slaughter of animals, which must be destructive to our morals."

(Nikola Tesla)

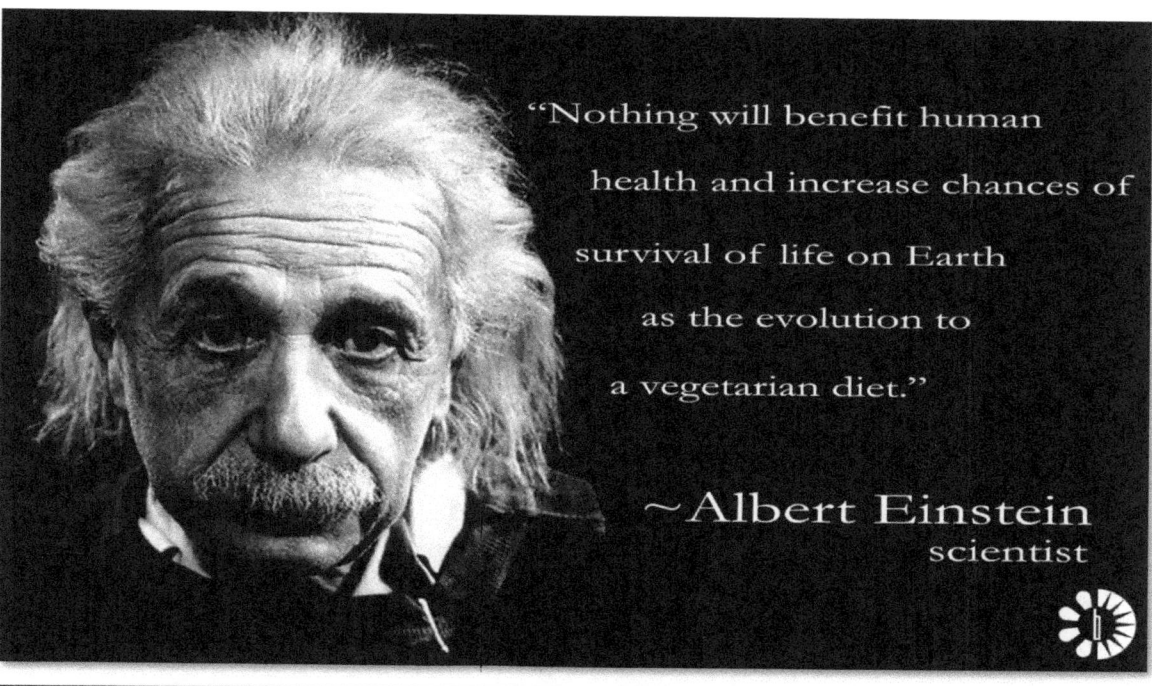

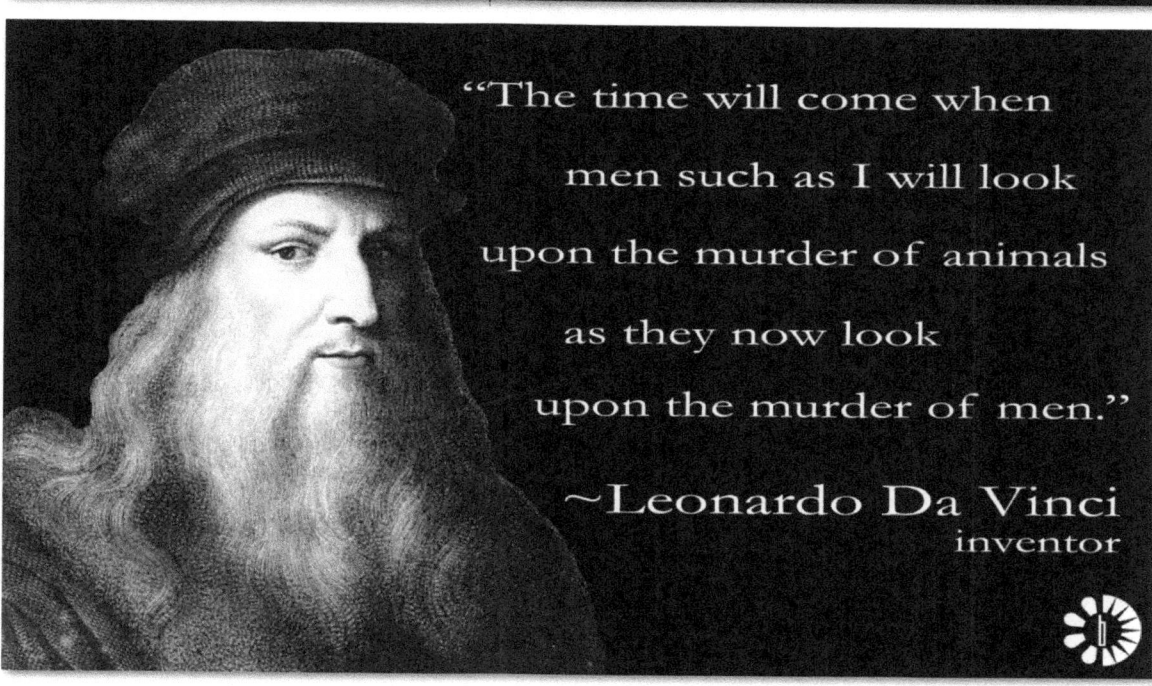

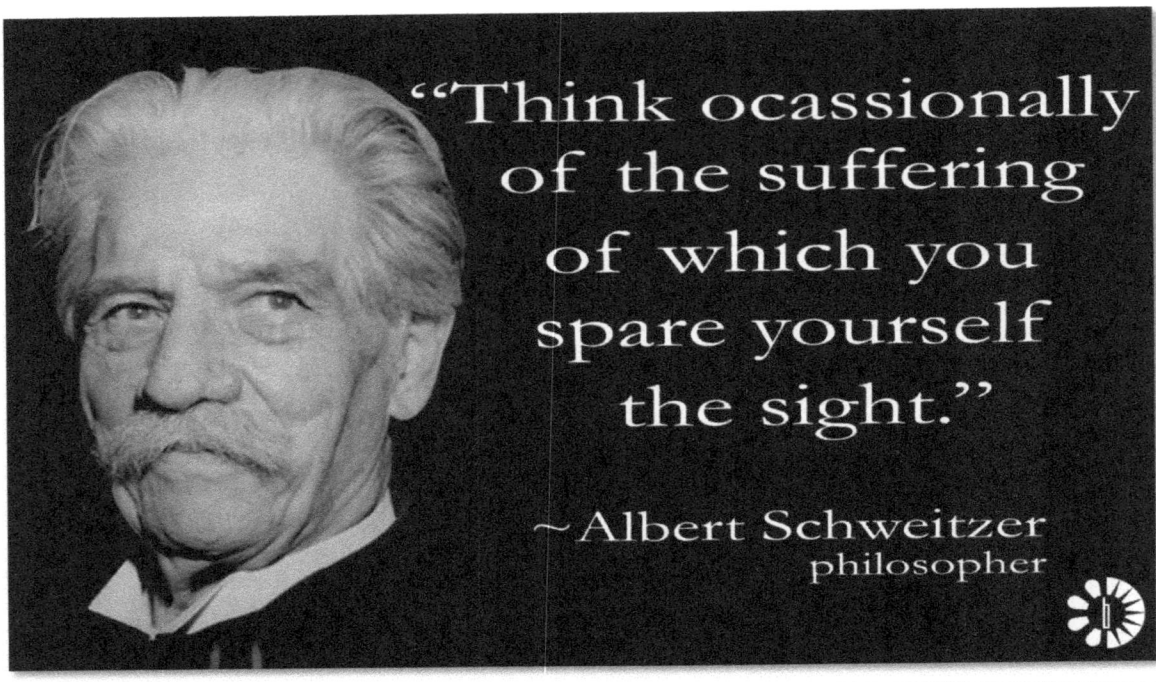

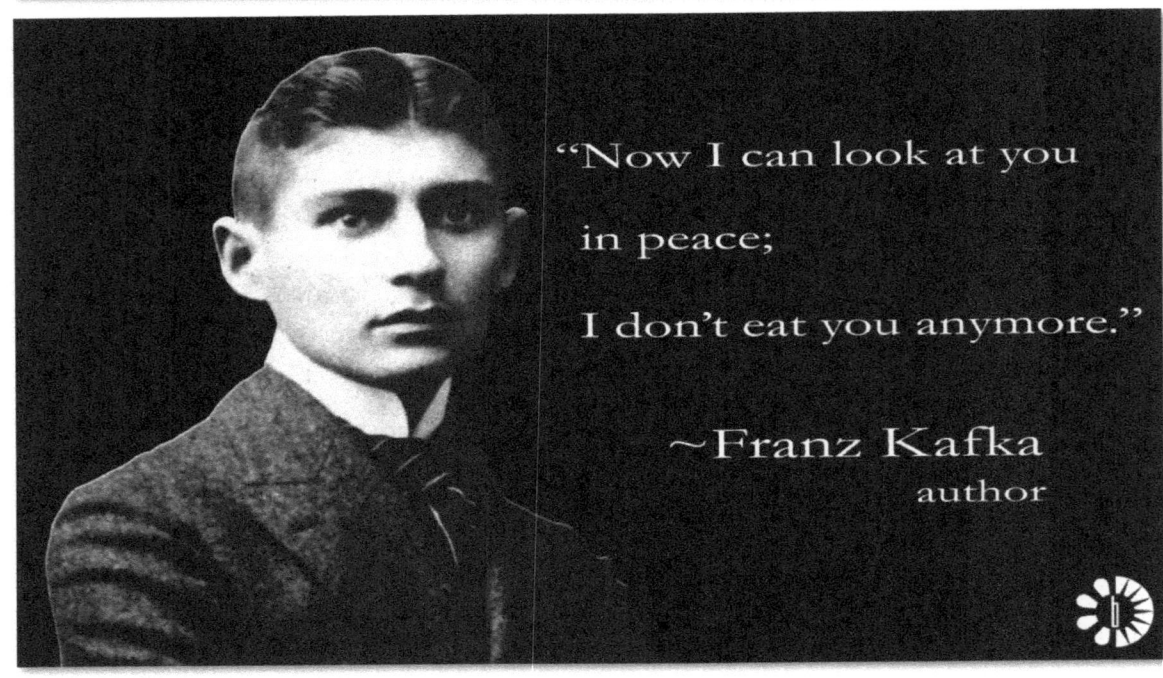

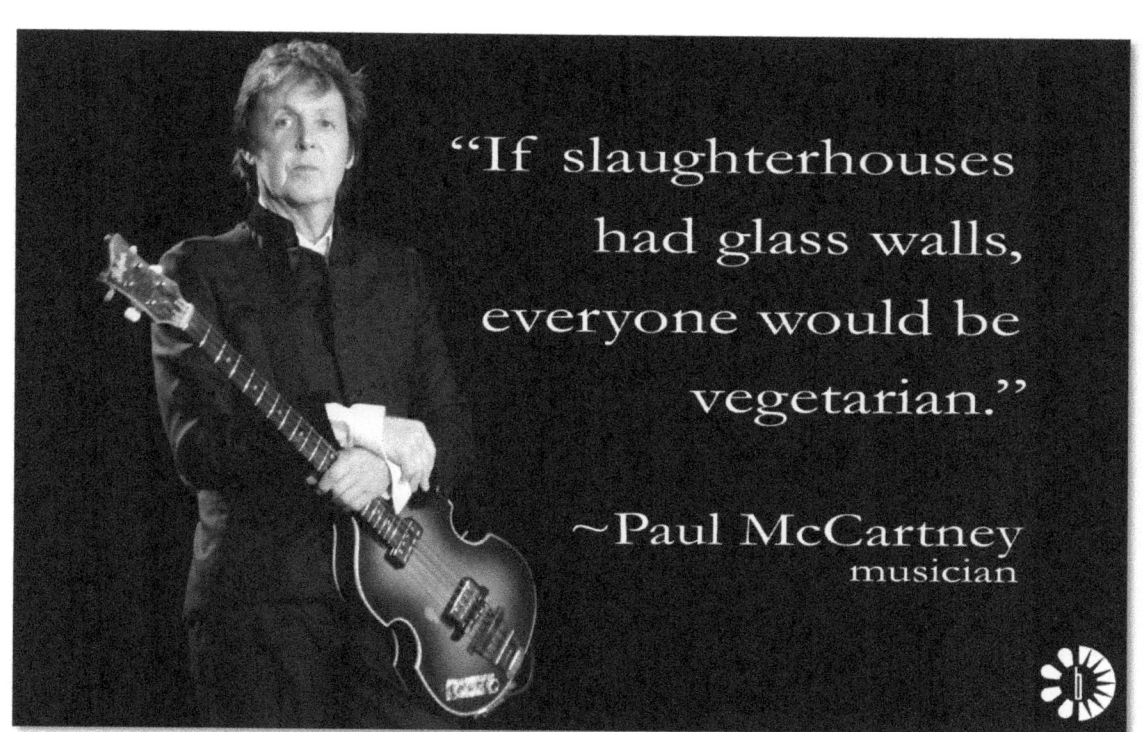

"For those who can feel,
no explanation is necessary.
For those who can't feel,
no explanation is ever good enough."

A & T Napoleon Foundation

Appendix

Ladies and gentlemen, I now invite you to meet a virus in all her 29,881-nucleotide glory, a virus that needs no introduction: the infamous SARS-CoV-2.

```
1 attaaaggtt tataccttcc caggtaacaa accaaccaac tttcgatctc ttgtagatct 61 gttctctaaa cgaacttta aatctgtgtg gctgtcactc
ggctgcatgc ttagtgcact 121 cacgcagtat aattaataac taattactgt cgttgacagg acacgagtaa ctcgtctatc 181 ttctgcaggc tgcttacggt
ttcgtccgtg ttgcagccga tcatcagcac atctaggttt 241 cgtccgggtg tgaccgaaag gtaagatgga gagccttgtc cctggtttca acgagaaaac 301
acacgtccaa ctcagtttgc ctgttttaca ggttcgcgac gtgctcgtac gtggctttgg 361 agactccgtg gaggaggtct tatcgaggc acgtcaacat
cttaaagatg gcacttgtgg 421 cttagtagaa gttgaaaaag gcgttttgcc tcaacttgaa cagccctatg tgttcatcaa 481 acgttcggat gctcgaactg
cacctcatgg tcatgttatg gttgagctgg tagcagaact 541 cgaaggcatt cagtacggtc gtagtggtga gacacttggt gtccttgtcc ctcatgtggg 601
cgaaatacca gtggcttacc gcaaggttct tcttcgtaag aacggtaata aaggagctgg 661 tggccatagt tacgcgccg atctaaagtc atttgactta
ggcgacgagc ttggcactga 721 tccttatgaa gatttttcaag aaaactggaa cactaaacat acagtggtg ttacccgtga 781 actcatgcgt gagcttaacg
gaggggcata cactcgctat gtcgataaca acttctgtgg 841 ccctgatggc taccctcttg agtgcattaa agaccttcta gcacgtgctg gtaaagcttc 901
atgcacttg tccgaacaac tggactttat tgacactaag aggggtgtat actgctgccg 961 tgaacatgag catgaaattg cttggtacac ggaacgttct
gaaaagagct atgaattgca 1021 gacacctttt gaaattaaat tggcaaagaa atttgacacc ttcaatgggg aatgtccaaa 1081 ttttgtattt cccttaaatt
ccataatcaa gactattcaa ccaagggttg aaagaaaaa 1141 gcttgatggc tttatgggta gaattcgatc tgtctatcca gttgcgtcac caaatgaatg 1201
caaccaaatg tgcctttcaa ctctcatgaa gtgtgatcat tgtggtgaaa cttcatgaag 1261 gacgggcgat tttgttaaag ccacttgcga attttgtggc
actgagaatt tgactaaaga 1321 aggtgccact acttgtggtt acttacccca aaatgctgtt gttaaaattt attgtccagc 1381 atgtcacaat tcagaagtag
gacctgagca tagtcttgcc gaataccata atgaactgg 1441 cttgaaaacc attcttcgta aggtggtcg cactattgcc tttggaggct gtgtgttctc 1501
ttatgttggt tgccataaca agtgtgccta ttgggttcca cgtgctagcg ctaacatagg 1561 ttgtaaccat acaggtgttg ttggagaagg ttccgaaggt
cttaatgaca accttcttga 1621 aatactccaa aaagagaaag tcaacatcaa tattgttggt gactttaaac ttaatgaaga 1681 gatcgccatt attttggcat
cttttctgc ttccacaagt gcttttgtgg aaactgtgaa 1741 aggtttggat tataaagcat tcaaacaaat tgttgaatcc tgtggtaatt taaagttac 1801
aaaaggaaaa gctaaaaag gtgcctggaa tattggtgaa cagaaatcaa tactgagtcc 1861 tcttattgca tttgcatcag aggctgctcg tgttgtacga
tcaatttct cccgcactct 1921 tgaaactgct caaattctg tgcgtgttt acagaaggcc gctataacaa tactagatg 1981 aatttcacag tattcactga
gactcattga tgctatgatg ttcacatctg atttggctac 2041 taacaatctg gttaatgg cctacattac aggtggtgtt gttcagttga cttcgcagtg 2101
gctaactaac atctttggca ctgtttatga aaaactcaaa cccgtccttg attggctgta 2161 agagaagttt aaggaaggtg tagagtttct tagagacggt
tgggaaattg ttaaatttat 2221 ctcaacctgt gcttgtgaaa ttgtcggtgg acaaattgtc acctgtgcaa aggaaattaa 2281 ggagagtgtt cagacattct
ttaagcttgt aaataaattt ttggctttgt gtgctgactc 2341 tatcattatt ggtggagcta aacttaaagc cttgaattta ggtgaaacat ttgtcacgca 2401
ctcaaaggga ttgtacagaa agtgtgttaa atccagagaa gaaactggcc tactcatgcc 2461 tctaaaagcc ccaaagaaa ttatcttctt agagggagaa
acacttccca cagaagtgtt 2521 aacagaggaa gttgtcttga aaactggtga tttacaacca ttagaacaac ctactagtga 2581 agctgttgaa gctccattgg
ttggtacacc agtttgtatt aacgggctta tggttgctcg 2641 atcaaagaac actgtgcct tgcacctaat atgatggtaa caaacaatac 2701
cttcacactc aaaggcggtg caccaacaaa ggttacttt ggtgatgaca ctgtgataga 2761 agtgcaaggt tacaagagtg tgaatatcac ttttgaactt
gatgaaagga ttgataaagt 2821 acttaatgag aagtgctctg cctatacagt tgaactcggt acagaagtaa atgagttcgc 2881 ctgtgtgtg gcagatgctg
tcataaaaac tttgcaacca gtatctgaat tacttacacc 2941 actcgggcatt gatttagatg agtggagtat ggctacatac tacttatttg atgagtcgg 3001
tgagtttaaa ttggcttcac atatgtattg ttcttttctac cctccagatg aggatgaaga 3061 agaaggtgat tgtgaagaag aagagtttga gccatcaact
caatatgagt atggtactga 3121 agatgattac caaggtaaac ctttggaatt tggtgccact tctgctgctc ttcaacctga 3181 agaagcaa gaagaagatt
ggttagatga tgatagtcaa caaactgtg gtcaaacaga 3241 cggcagtgag gaacactcac aaccaactat tcaaaacatt gttgaggttc aacctcaatt 3301
agagatggaa cttacaccag ttgttcagac tattgaagtg aatagttatt 3361 aaaacttact gacaatgtat acattaaaaa tgcagacatt
gtggaagaag ctaaaaaggt 3421 aaaaccaaca gtggttgtta atgcagccaa tgtttacctt aaacatgag gaggtgttgc 3481 aggagcctta aataaggcta
ctaacaatgc catgcaagtt gaatctgatg attacatagc 3541 tactaatgga cccttaaagg tgggtggtt ttgtgtttta agcggacaca atcttgctaa 3601
acactgtctt catgttgtcg gcccaaatgt taacaaaggt gaagcattc aacttcttaa 3661 gagtgcttat gaaaatttta atcagcacga agttctactt
gcaccattat tatcagctgg 3721 tattttttgt gctgacccta tacatttctt aagagttttgt gtagatactg ttcgcaaaa 3781 tgtctactta gctgtctttg
ataaaaatct ctatgcaaaa cttgttcaa gctttttgga 3841 aatgaagagt gaaaagcaag ttgaacaaaa gatcgctgag attcctaaag aggaagttaa 3901
gccatttata actgaaagta aaccttcagt gaacagagaa aaacaagtat aagaaat 3961 caaagcttgt gttgaagaag ttaacaacac tctggaagaa
actaagttcc tcacagaaaa 4021 cttgttactt tatattgaca ttaatggac tcttcatca gattctgcca ctcttgttag 4081 tgacattgac atcactttct
taaagaaaga tgctccatat agtgggtgg atgttgttca 4141 agagggtgtt ttaactgctg tggttatacc tactaaaaag gctgagtgca ctactgaaat 4201
gctagcgaaa gctttgaaa aagtgccaac agacaattat ataaccactt acccgggtca 4261 gggtttaaat ggttacactg tagaggaggc aaagacagtg
cttaaaaagt gtaaaagtgc 4321 cttttacatt ctaccatcta ttatctcta tgagaagcaa gaaattcttg gaactgttc 4381 ttggaatttg cgagaaatgc
ttgcacatgc agaagaaaca cgcaaattga tgcctgtcg 4441 tgtgaaact aaagccatag tttcaactat acagcgtaaa tataaggta ttaaaataca 4501
agagggtgtg gttgattatg gtgctagatt ttacttttac accagtaaaa caactgtagc 4561 gtcacttatc aacacactta acgatctaaa tgaaactctt
gttacaatgc cacttggctcca 4621 tgtaacacat ggcttaaatt tggaagaagc tgctcggtat atgagatctc tcaaagtgcc 4681 agctacagtt tctgttttctt
cacctgatgc tgttacagcg tataatggtt atctcacttc 4741 ttcttctaaa acacctgaag aacattttat tgaaaccatc tcacttgctg gttcctataa 4801
agattggtcc tattctggac aatctacaca actaggtata gaatttctta gagaggtga 4861 taaaagtgta tattcacta gtaatcctac cacattccca
ctagatggtg aagttatcac 4921 ctttgacaat cttaagccag aggaaggtg aggactatta aggtgtttac 4981 aacagtgac aacataacc
tccacacga agttgtggac atgtcaatga catatgacaa 5041 acagttggt ccaacttatt tggatggagc tgatgttact aaaaataaac ctcataattc 5101
acatgaaggt aaaactttg atgtttataa tgatgacact ctacgtg tgaggcttt 5161 tgagactac cacacaactg atcctagttc tctgggatagg
tacatgcatg cattaaatca 5221 cactaaaaag tggaataca tagttttact tgggtaaagt tctattaaat gggcagataa 5281 caactgttat cttgccactg
cattgttaac actccaacaa atagatgta agtttaatcc acctgctcta caagatgctt attacagaca aagggctggt gaagctgcta actttgtgc 5401
acttatcta gcctactgta aataacagt aggtgagtta ggtgatgtta gagaaaacat 5461 gagttacttg tttcaacatg ccaatttaga ttccttgcaaa
agagtcttga acgtggtgtg 5521 taaaactgt ggacaacagc agacaaccct taaggtgta tgtacatggg 5581 cacctttct tatgaacaat
ttaagaaagg tgttcagata ccttgtacgt gtggtaaaca 5641 agctacaaa tatctagtac aacaggagtc accttttgtt atgatgtcag caccacctgc 5701
tcagtaatga ctttaaggcatg gtacattca ttgtgcgagt gagtacagtg gtaattcatcc 5761 gtgtggtcac tataaacata taacttctaa agaaacttg
tatttgcatag acggtgcttt 5821 acttaacaag tcctcaaat acaaagctgc ctattctgtttctaca aagaaaactgtt ttcacaca accatacaaaac 
cagttactta taaattggat ggtgttgttt gtacagaaat 5941 tgacccttaag ttgacaatt attataagaa agaacattctt tatttcacag agcaaccaat 6001
tgatcttgta ccaaccaac catatccaaa cgcaagctc gataatttt agttgtatg 6061 tgataatact aattttgctg atgtattca ccagtaact
ggttataaga aacctgcttc 6121 aagagagctta aagttacat tttcccctga cttaaattgt gatgtggtg ctattgatta 6181 taaacactac acaccctctt
ttaagaaagg agctaaattg ttacataaac ctattgtttg gcatgttaac aatgcaacta 6241 ataaagccac gtataaacca aatacctggt gtatacgttg 6301
tcttttggagc acaaaaccag ttgaaacatc aaattgttt gatgtactga gtcagagta 6361 cgcgcaggga atggatcatgc ttgactcgcga agatcaaaa
ccagtctctg aagaagtag 6421 ggaaatcct accatcaga aagacgtttc tgactgtaat gtgaaacta ccgaagtgt 6481 aggagacatt acttttaaac
cagcaaataa tagttaaaaa attacagaag aggttggcca 6541 cacagatcta atggctgctg ataagcaa tcaatgcag aacagctgtc 6601
attatctaga gttgcttggtg tgaaaccct tgctctatgc tgttttaat tggtcttggt 6661 tgtctccttg gactacagtg ctaattatgc taagccttttt
cttaacaaag ttgttatagac 6721 aacctacaac atagttcaa ggtgtttaaa ccgttttgc acaatataa tgccttattt 6781 ctttacttct ttgctacaat
tgtgtacttt tactagaagt acaaattcta aatataaagc 6841 atctcatgcg actacatag caagaatac tgttaagt gtcggtaaat tttgtcctaga 6901
ggcttcattt aatatatgta gtcaccatcta taatttttga gttttactta ttaggtttt 6961 gttttaccta ttaaggtttt gcctaggttc tttaatctac
tcaaccgctg ctttaggtgt 7021 tttaatgtct atttttgcgg tgcttctta ctgtactggt tacagaaag gcatttaga 7081 ctctactaat gtcactattg
caacctactg tactggtctt atccttgta gtgttgtct 7141 tagtggttta gatcttag acctatcc ttcttaga actatacaa ttaccattc 7201
atctttaa tgggatta ctgctttgg tagtttagta gcctatata acgcatgttt 7261 tctttccac aggttttct atgtacttgt attggctgca
atcatgcaat tgtttttcag 7321 ctattttaca gtactttta ttaatttgg ctttttatg gttaataa ttactttgt 7381 acaaatggcc ccgaatcag
ctatggttag aatgtacatc ttcttccat cattttatta 7441 tgtatggaaa gtatgatg atgttgtaga cggtgttaat tcatcaactt gttagatgtg 7501
ttacaaacgt aatagagaca agaggccga atgtactgtt tggataagaa ttagaggcatc 7561 gtcctttat gtctctatag atgagggatg ataggagtcc
aaactacaca attggaattg 7621 tgttaattgct gatacattc gtgctgtag tacatttat gtgatgaag ttgcgagaga 7681 ctttgcacta cagtttaaa
gaccaataaa tcctactgac cagtcttct acatcgtga 7741 tagtgttaca gtgaagaatg gttccatcca ttttactttt gataaagctg tcaaagacgc 7801
ttatgaaaa ccattctct ctcattttgt taacttaat caaaacttta cattaaattc 7861 taaagttgcc tacaacaaatg cttgaatgca ttaaaagtaat
aaatcaaaat gtgaagaatc 7921 atctgcaaaa tcagcgtcta tttactacag tcagcttatg tgtcaaccta ctgttact 7981 agatcaggca ttagtgctcg
atgttggta tagtgcggaa gttgcagtta aatgttta 8041 tgcttacgtt aatacgtttt catcaacttt taacgtacca atggaaaaac tcaaaacact
agttgcaact gcagaagctg aacttgcaaa gaatgtgtcc ttagacaatg tcttatctac 8161 ttttatttca gcagctcggc aaggggttgt tgatcagat
```

131

```
       gtagaaacta aagatgttgt 8221 gaatgtcett aaattgtcac atcaatctga catgaaagtt actggcgata gttgtaataa 8281 ctatatgctc acctataaca
aagttgaaaa catgacaccc cgtgacctig gtgcttgtat 8341 tgactgtagt gcgcgtcata ttaatgcgca ggtagcaaaa agtcacaaca ttgctttgat 8401
atgaacgtt aaagattca tgtcattgtc tgaacaacta cgaaacaaa tacgtagtgc 8461 tgctaaaaag aataacttac cttttaagtt gacatgtgca
actactagac aagttgttaa 8521 tgttgtaaca acaaagatag cacttaaggg tggtaaaatt gttaaataatt ggtgaagca 8581 gttaattaaa gttacacttg
tgttcctttt tgttgctgct attttctatt taataacacc 8641 tgttcatgtc atgtctaaac atactgactt ttcaagtgaa atcataggat acaaggctat 8701
tgatggtggt gtcactcgtg acatagcatc tacagatact tgttttgcta acaaacatgc 8761 tgattttgac acatgtttta gccagcgtgg tggtagttat
actaatgaca aagcttgccc 8821 attgattgca tgcagttata gcagtcataa caagagaagt gggtttttgtc gtgctggtt tgcctggcac 8881 gatattacgc acaactaatg
gtgacttttt gcatttctta cctagagttt ttagtgcatt 8941 tggtaacatc tgttacacac catcaaaact tatagagtac actgactttg caacatcagc 9001
ttgtgtttg gctgctgaat gtacaattt taaagatgct tctggtaagc cagtaccata 9061 ttgttatgat accaatgtac tagaaggttc tgttgcttat
gaaagtttac gccctgactc 9121 acgttatgtg ctcatggatg gctctattat tcaatttcct aacacctacc 9181 ttgaaggttc tgttagagtg gtaacaactt
ttgattctga gtactgtagg cacggcactt gtgaaagatc 9241 agaagctggt gttttgtgtat ctactagtgg tagatgggta cttaacaatg attattacag 9301
atctttacca ggagtttct gtggtgtaga tgctgtaaat ttacttaca atatgtttac 9361 accataatt caacctattg gtgctttgga catatcagca
tctatagtag ctggtggtat 9421 tgtagctatc agcttgaaat gccttgccta ctatttatg aggtttagaa gagcttttgg 9481 tgaatacagt catgtagttg
cctttaatac tttactattc cttatgtcat tcactgtact 9541 ctgtttaaca ccagtttact cattcttacc tggtgtttat tctgttattt acttgtactt 9601
gacatttat cttactaatg atgttcttt tttagcacat attcagtgga tgttatgt 9661 cacaccttta gtaccttct ggataacaat tgcttatatc
atttgtattt ccacaaagca 9721 tttctattgg ttctttagta attacctaaa gagacgtgta gtcttaatg gtgttcctt 9781 tagtactttt gaagaagctg
cgctgtgcac ctttttgtta aataaagaa tgtatctaaa 9841 gttgcgtagt gatgtgctat tacctcttac gcaatataat agatacttag ctctttataa 9901
taagtacaga tattttagtg gagcaatgga tacaactagc tacagagaag ctgcttgttg 9961 tcatctcgca aaggctctca atgacttcag taacttcagt
tctgatgttc tttaccaacc 10021 accacaaacc tctatccacct cagctgtttt gcagagtggt ttagaaaaaa tggcattccc 10081 atctgtaaa
gttgagggtt gtatggtaca agtaacttgt ggtacaacta cacttaacgg 10141 tcttttgcttt gatgacgtag ttactgtcc aagacatgtg atctgcacct
ctgaagacat 10201 gcttaaccct aattatgaag atttactcat tcgtaagtct aatcataatt tcttggtaca 10261 ggctggtaat gttcaactca
gggttattgg acattcgtat caaaattgtg tacttaagtg 10321 taaggttgaa acagccaatc ctaagacacc taagtataag tttgttcgca ttcaaccagg
10381 acagacttt tcagtgttaa cttgttacaa tggttcacca tctggtgttt accaatgtgc 10441 tatgaggccc aatttcacta ttaagggttc
attccttaat ggttcatgtg gtagtgttgg 10501 ttttaacata gattatgact gtgtctcttt ttgttacatg caccatatgg aattaccaac 10561
tggagttcat gctggcacag acttagaagg taacttttat ggacctttg ttgacagtga 10621 aacagcacaa gcagctggta cggacacaac tattacagtt
aatgttttag cttggtttgta 10681 cgctgctgtt ataaatggag acaggtggtt tctcaatcga tttaccacaa ctcttaatga 10741 ctttaacctt
gtggctatga agtacaatta tgaacctcta acacaagacc atgttgaaat 10801 actaggacct ctttctgctc aaactggaat tgccgttttta gatatgtgtg
cttcattaaa 10861 agaattactg caaaatgta tgaatgacg taccatattg ggtagtgctt tattagaaga 10921 tgaatttaca cctttgatg
ttgttagaca atgctcaggt gttacttcc aagtgcagt 10981 gaaaagaaca atcaaggta cacaccctg gttgttactc acaatttga cttcactttt
11041 agttttagtc cagatgactc aagtgtgtt gttctttttt ttgtatgaaa atgcctttt tgtaactgtt 11101 aacttttgct atgggtatta ttgctatgtc
tgctttttgca atgatgtttt tcaaacataa 11161 gcatgcattt ctctgtttgt ttttgttacc ttcttcttgcc actgtagctt attttaatt 11221
ggtctatatg cctgctagtt gggtgatgcg tattatgaca tggttggata tggttgatac 11281 tagttttgtct ggttttaagc taaaagactg tgttatgtat
gcatcagctg tagtgttact 11341 aatccttatg acagcaagaa ctgtgatagt tgatggtget aggaagtgt ggacacttat 11401 gaatgtctg
acactcgttt ataaagttta ttatggtaat gctttagatc aagccattgc 11461 catgtgggct cttataatct ctgttacttc taactactca ggtgtagtta
caactgtcat 11521 gttttggcc agaggtattg ttttatgtg tgttgagtat tgcccttt tcttcataac 11581 tggtaataca cttcagtgta
taattgtctt ttattgttc ttaggtctatt tttgtacttg ttacttgc 11641 ttactttgcc tactcaaccg ctactttga ctgactcgtg gtgtttatga
11701 ttacttagtt tctcacacag agttagata tatgaattca cagggactac tcccaccaa 11761 gaatagcata gatgccttca aactcaacat
acttcagtt ttgcaacaac tcagagtaga atcatcatct aaattgtggg 11821 tatcaaagta gccactgtac agtcaaaat gtcagatgta aagtgcacat cagtagtctt 11881
gaagcctttg aaaaaatggt 12001 ttcactactt tctgttttgc tttccatgca gggtgctgta gacataaaca agctttgtga 12061 agaaatgctg
ctaatggtga 12181 ttctgaagtt gttcttaaaa agttgaagaa gtcttttgaat gtggctaaat ctgaatttga 12241 ccgtgatgca gccatgcaac
gtaagttgga aaagatggc gatcaagcta tgacccaaat 12301 gtataaacag ctagatcg aggacaagag gcaaagtt actagtgcta tgcagacaat
12361 gcttttttcact atgcttagaa agttggataa tgatgcactc aacaacatta tcaacaatgc 12421 aagagatgct tgtgttccct tgaactataat
acctcttaca acagcagcca aactaatgct 12481 tgtcatacac gactataaca catataaaa tacgtgtgat ggtacaacact ttacttatgc 12541
atcagcatta tggggaaatc aacaggttgt agatgcagat agtaaaattc ttcaacttag 12601 tgaaattagt atggacaatt cacctaattt agcatggcct
cttattgtaa cagctttaag 12661 ggcaattct gctgtcaaat tacagaataa tgagcttagt cctgttgcac tacgacagat 12721 gtcttgtgct
gccggtacta cacaaactgc ttgcactgat gacaatgcgt tagctactac 12781 caacacaaca aggggaggta ggttttgtact tgcactgtta tccgatttac
aggatttgaa 12841 atgggctaga ttccctaaga gtgatggaac tggtactatc tatacagaac tggaaccacc 12901 ttgtaggtttt gttacagaca
cacttaaagg tcctaaagta aagtatttat acttttataga aggattaaac aacctcaaata 12961 aggattaaac aacctaaata gagtgttaac ttggtagt ttagctgcca catacgtct
13021 acaagctggt aatgcaacag aagtgcttgc caattcaact gtattatctc tctgtgcttt 13081 tgctgtagat gctgctaaag cttacaaga
ttatcagct agtggggac aaccaatcac 13141 taattgtgtt aagatgtgt gtacacacac tggtactgtg caggcaataa cagttacacc 13201
ggaagccaat atggatcaag aatccttaag tgggtcatcg tgttgtctc actgggtttc 13261 ccacatagat catccaaatc ctaaaggatt tgttgactta
aaaggtaagt atgtacaaat 13321 acctacaact tgtgctaatg accctgtgg ttttaacatt aaaaacacag tctgtaccgt 13381 ctgcggatgt
tggtaaaaggtt atgggctagt tgtgatcaa ctccgcgaac ccatgcttca 13441 gacacgtggt gcaagctgat gcacaatcgt ttttaaacgg gttgcggtg taagtgcagc
ccgtcttaca 13501 ccgtgcggca caggacctac tactgatgtc gtatacaggg cttttgact ctacaatgat 13561 aaagtagctg gttttgctaa
attcctaaaa actaattgtt gtcgcttcca agaaaaggac 13621 gaagatgaca atttaattga ttcttacttt gtagttaaga gacacacttt ctcaactaac
13681 caacatgaag aacaattta taattttactt aaggattgc cagctgttttgc taacagtact 13741 ttcttttaagt ttagaataga cggtgacatg
gtaccacata tatcacgtca acgtcttaca 13801 aaatacacaa tggcagacct cgtctatgct ttaaggcatt ttgatgaagt taattgtgac 13861
acattaaaag aaatacttgt cacatacaat tgttgtgatg atgattatt caataaaaag 13921 gactggtatg atttttgtaga aaacccagat atattacgcg
tatacgccaa cttaggtgaa 13981 cgtgtacgcc aagctttgt aaaaacaata caattctgtg atgccatgcg aaatgctggt 14041 attgttggtg
tactgacatt agataatcaa gatctcaatg gtaactgtta tgatttcggt 14101 gattttcatc aaacccacgcc aggtagtgga gttcctgttg tagattctta
ttattcattg 14161 ttaatgcta tattaacctt gaccaggggt ttaactgcag agtcacatgt tgacactgac 14221 ttaacaaagc cttacattaa
gtgggatttg acttcacgga aagaaggtta 14281 aaactctgt accgttatt taatatttg aagcatcagac accacccaaa ttgtgttaac
14341 tgtttggatg acagatgat tctgcattgt gcaaactta atgtttattt ctctacagtg 14401 ttcccaccta caagttttgg acctatgtg
agaaaaatat tgttgatgg tgttccatttg 14461 gtagttcaa ctggataca cttcagaag ctggtgttg tacataatca ggatgtaaac 14521
ttacatagct ctagacttag ttttaagaa ttacttgtat atgctgcgta ccctgctatg 14581 cacgctgctt ctggtaatct attaccagat aaagcgcacta
cgtgcttttc agtagctgca 14641 cttaactaaca atgttgcttt tcaaactgtc aaacccgcgta attttaacaa agactttctat 14701 gacttgctg
tgtctaaggg ttttcttaag gaaggagtt ctgttgaat aaaacacttg 14761 ttctttgcct aggatgaat tgctgctatc agcgattag actactatcg
ttataatcta 14821 ccaacaatgt gtagatgaca caactacta tttagttg aagtacttt 14881 gattgttaacg atggttggcgtg
tattaatgct aaccaagtca tcgtcaacaa ccctagacaa tcagctggtt ttccattata 14941 taaatgggg aaggctagac tttattatga ttcaatgagt
15001 tatgaggatc aagatgcact tttcgcatat acaaaacgta atgtcatccc tactataact 15061 caaatgaat ctatgacctca cattagtgca
aagaataagag ctcgcaccgt agctgctgtc 15121 tctctgcta gtagtaatga caatagcaat tttcatcaaa aattattgaa ctcaaatgcc 15181
gccactagag gagctactgt agtaattgga acaacgaaat tctatggtggt ttggcacaac 15241 atgtaaaaa tctgtttttag tgaatgtgtgaa aaccctcacc
ttatgggttg gggattatcct 15301 aaatgtgata gagccatgcc taacatgct agaattatgg cctcactttgt tcttctgcgc 15361 aaacatacaa
cgtgttgtag cttgtcacac cgtttctata gattagctaa tggtggtcac 15421 tttttcaaga gtgaagtgat catgtggtgc ggtcactat gttaaacc
aggtggaacc 15481 tcatccaggag atgccacaac tgcttatgct aatagtgttt ttaacattt tgccaagctgtc 15541 acggccaaatg ttaatgcact
tttatctact gatggtaaca aaaattgccga taagtatgcc 15601 cgcaatttac aacacagcct tatgagtgt tctctagaaa atagagatgt tgacacagac
15661 ttttgtgaatg agttttgctt aatatttgt aaacattttc caatatgtct attacgtgac 15721 gatgctgttg tgtgttttaa tagcacttat
gcatctcaag gtcagtggcc tagcataaga 15781 aactttaaag cagttcttta ttatcaaaaca atgtttta tgtctgaagc aaaatgtttgg 15841
actgagactg accttactaa aggaccttaa gaatttttgt ctcaacatac aagctgttga 15901 ttaaactgag atgaggtgga agttagatta ccccagatc
catcaagaat ctcaggggcc 15961 ggctgttttg tagatgatat cgtaaaaaca gatgtgtcac ttatgattga acggtcgtg 16021 tctttcagcta
tagatgctta cccactacct aaacatccta atcaggagta tgctgatgtc 16081 tttcatttgt acttacaata cagaaaag cttacatgag agttaacagg
acacatgtta 16141 gacatgctt ctgttatgct tcaataagt aacaacagcct ggtattggga acctcaggtt 16201 tatggaggta tgtacacacc
gcatcagtgc ttacaggtc ttgggggtcag gttcttttgc 16261 aattcacaga cttcattaag atgtggtgt tgcatacggta gaccattcatt atgttgtaaa
16321 tgctgttacg accatgtcat atcaactaca cataaattag tcttgtctgt taatcgctat 16381 gttgaatgtg ctccaggtgt tgatgtcaca
gatgtgactc aacttcatct aggtgatatg 16441 agctattatt gtaaaccaca taagttttc cattgtcatc caggtcagttg tgaaagaatc
gtttttgct tatatttaaa tacatgtct agtcatgctgt cgatttaata gttttcataaaaca 16561 attgcaacat gtgacggcca aaatgctggt gatcacatt
tagctaacac ctgtactgaa 16621 agactcaagc ttttgcagc agaaacgtc aaagctactg aggagacatt taactgtct 16681 tatggtatig
ctactacgcg tctgcagca caggaactag tacttgcctg gtaagctgcc ttgtcttgtct 16741 tcatgggaa ctagaccacc acttaaccga aattatgtct
tcgtaact 16801 aaaaaacaga aagtaaaat agggaagtac acctttggaa aaagtgacta tggttgtaac 16861 gttgtttac gaggtacaac
aacttacaaa ttaatgtgtg gtgattattt tgtcgtgaca 16921 tcacatacag taatgccatt aagtgcacct acactagtgc cacaagagca ctatgttaga
16981 attactgtct tatcccaac actcaatcta tcagatggct ttcctagcaa ccttaatggg 17041 tatcaaagg ttggatgca aagtattct
acactccagtg gaccacctga tactgggtaag 17101 agtcattttg ctattggccct agctctctac acccctctg ctccgcatagt gtatacagct 17161
tgctctcatg ccgctcgttga tgcactatgt gagaagcgat taaaatattt gcctatagat 17221 aaatgtagta gaattatacc tgcacgtgct cgtgtagagt
```

```
            gttttgataa attcaaagtg 17281 aattcaacat tagaacagta tgtcttttgt actgtaaatg cattgcctga gacgacagca 17341 gatatagttg
            tctttgatga aatttcaatg gccacaaatt atgatttgag tgttgtcaat 17401 gccagattac gtgctaagca ctatgtgtac attgcgacc  ctgctcaatt
            acctgcacca 17461 cgcacattgc taactaaggg cacactagaa ccagaatatt tcaattcagt gtgtagactt 17521 atgaaaacta taggtccaga
            catgttcctc ggaacttgtc ggcgttgtcc tgctgaaatt 17581 gttgacactg tgagtgcttt ggtttatgat aataagctta aagcacataa agacaaatca
            17641 gctcaatgct ttaaaatgtt ttataagggt gttatcacgc atgatgtttc atctgcaatt 17701 aacaggccac aaataggcgt ggtaagagaa
            ttccttacac gtaaccctgc ttggagaaaa 17761 gctgtcttta tttcacctta taattcacag aatgctgtag cctcaaagat tttgggacta 17821
            ccaactcaaa ctgttgattc atcacagggc tcagaatatg actatgtcat attcactcaa 17881 accactgaaa cagctcactc ttgtaatgta aacagattta
            atgttgctat taccagagca 17941 aaagtaggca tactttgcat aatgtctgat agagaccttt atgacaagtt gcaatttaca 18001 agtcttgaaa
            ttccacgtag gaatgtggca actttacaag ctgaaaatgt aacaggactc 18061 tttaaagatt gtagtaaggt aatcactggg ttacatccta cacaggcacc
            tacacacctc 18121 agtgttgaca ctaaattcaa aactgaaggt ttatgtgttg acatacctgg tcatcctaag 18181 gacatgacct atagaagact
            catctctatg atgggttta aaatgaatta tcaagttaat 18241 ggttacccta acatgtttat cacccgcgaa gaagctataa gacatgtacg tgcatggatt
            18301 ggcttcgatg tcgagggttg tcatgctact agagaaagctg ttggtaccaa tttaccttta 18361 cagctaggtt tttctacagg tgttaaccta
            gttgctgtac ctacagttga tgtgataca 18421 cctaataata cctaataata cagatttttc cagagttagt gctaaaccac cgcctggaga tcaatttaaa 18481
            cacctcatac cacttgtat caaaggactt ccttggaatg tagtgcgtat aaagattgta 18541 caaatgttaa gtgacacact taaaatctc tctgacagag
            tcgtatttgt cttatgggca 18601 catggcttg agttgacatc tatgaagtat tttgtgaaaa taggacctga gcgcacctgt 18661 tgtctatgtg
            atagacgtgc cacatgcttt tccactgctt cagacactta tgcctgttgg 18721 catcattcta ttggattga ttacgtctat aatccgttca tgattgatgt
            tcaacaatgg 18781 ggttttacag gtaacctaca aagcaaccat gatctgtatt gtcaagtcca tggtaatgca 18841 catgtagcta gttgtgatgc
            aatcatgact aggttgtctag ctgtccacga gtgcttgtt tgttgactat 18901 aagcgtgttg actggactat tgaatatcct ataattggtg atgaactgaa gattaatgcg
            18961 gcttgtagaa aggttcaaca catggttgtt aaagctgcat tattagcaga caaattccca 19021 gttcttcacg acattggtaa ccctaaagct
            attaagtgtg tacctcaagc tgatgtagaa 19081 tggaagttct atgatgcaca gcctgtagt gacaaagctt ataaatagaa gaattattc  19141
            tattctttatg ccacacattc tgacaaattc acagatgtgtg tatgcctatt ttggaattgc 19201 aatgtcgata gatatcctgc taattccatt gtttgtagat
            ttgacactag agtgctactc 19261 aaccttaact tgcctggttg tgatgtggc agtttgtatg taaataaaca tgcattccac 19321 acaccagctc
            ttgataaaag tgctttgttt aatttaaaac aattaccatt tttctattac 19381 tctgacagtc catgtgagtc tcatggaaaa caagtagtgt cagatataga
            ttatgtacca 19441 ctaaagtctg ctacgtgtat aacacgttgc aatttaggtg gtgcttatgt tacagcatcat 19501 gctaatgagt acagattgta
            tctcgatgct tataacatga tgatctcagc tggctttaag 19561 tggtgggttt acaaacaatt tgatactat aacctctgga acacttttac aagacttcag
            19621 agtttagaaa atgtggcttt taatgttgta aataaggac  actttgatgg acacagggt 19681 gaagtaccag tttctcatcat taataacact
            gtttacacaa aagttgatgg tgttgacgta 19741 gaattgttga aaaataaac aacattaact gcaaaggtag cattggacct ttgggctaag 19801
            cgcaacatta aaccagtacc agaggtgaaa atactccaata atttgggtgt ggacattgc  19861 gctaatactg tgatctggga ctacaaaaga gatgctccag
            cacatatatc tactattggt 19921 gtttgttcta tgactgacat agccaagaaa ccaactgaaa cgatttgtgc accactcact 19981 gtcttttgtg
            atggtcaa gtgagacttat ggaaaatgc ccgtaagtgt 20041 gttcttatta cagaaggtag tgttaaagct ttacaaccat ctgtaggtcc
            caaacaagct 20101 agtcttaatg gagtcacatt aattggagaa gccgtaaaa cacagttcaa ttattatag  20161 aaagttgatg tgtttgtcca
            acaattacct gaaacttact ttactcagag tagaaattta 20221 caagaattta aacccaggag tcaaatgaa attgattcct tagaattagc tatggatgaa
            20281 ttcattgaac ggtataaatt agaaggtat gccttcgaac atcgtttta tggaatttta 20341 agtcatagtc agttaggtgg tttacatcta
            ctgattggac tagctaaacg ttttaaggaa 20401 tcacctttgg aattagaaga ttttattcct atggacacta cagtaaaaaa ctatttccata 20461
            acagatgcgc aaacaggttc atctgaaggt gtgtgttcta ttattgattt attacttgat 20521 gatttgttg aaataataaa atcccaagat ttatctgtag
            tttctaaggt tgtcaaagtg 20581 actattgact atacagaaat tcattatatg cttggtgta aagatgcca tgtagaaaca 20641 tttttacccaa
            aattacaatc tagtcaagcg tggcaaccgg gtgttgctat gcctaatctt 20701 tacaaaatgc aaagaatgct attagaaag  tgtgaccttc aaaattatgg
            tgatagtgca 20761 acattaccca agcataat gatgaatgtc gcaaaatca tcactgtg tcaatattta 20821 aacacattaa cattagctgt
            accctataat atgagagatta tactttggta tgctggttct 20881 gataaaggag ttgcaccagg tacagctgtt taagacagt agttgcctac gggtacgctg
            20941 cttgtcgatt cagatcttaa tgacttgtc tctgatcag attcaactt  gattggtgat 21001 tgtgcaactg tacatacagc taataaatg
            gatctcatta ttagtgatat gtacgaccct 21061 aagcagtcca ctaaaaatg tgatcaaaga aaaagaggtg ttcttaaag gttttttac ttacatttgt 21121
            ggttttatac aacaaaagct agctcttgga ggttccgtg ctataaagat aacagaacta 21181 tcttggaatg ctgatcttca taagctcatg ggacacttcg
            catggtggac agcctttgtt 21241 actaatgtga atgcgtcatc atctgaagca ttttttaattg gatgtaatta tcttggcaaa 21301 ccacggcaaac
            aaatagatgt ttatgtcatg catgcaaatt acatattttg gaggaataca 21361 aatccaaattc agttgtctc  ctatctttca tttgacatga gtaaagtcc
            cctttaaatta 21421 agggtactg ctgttgtgc ttttaaagaa ggtcaaatca atgatatgat tttatctct  cttagtaaag gtagacttat
            aattagagaa aacaacagag ttgttatttc tagtgatgtt 21541 cttgttaaca actaaacgaa caatgtttgt ttttcttgtt ttattgccac tagtctctag
            21601 tcagtgtgtt aatcttacaa ccagaactca aattaccct gatacttacg ttaccccctg 21661 ttattaccct tgaccttccc tcaaacagtt ttaccccgtt
            gttaaagact ttcacccaca acctcaacaa 21721 tcaaattaaa attacattctg ttaagaaat tttggtctaa ctggtaaaga atttcgcact ttatgcggaa
            cctttggtag atctcaacca agtggtgaca tggtccatcc atgaaaagcc ttgaaagttg atccttgaca tgaatcacct aaaaaatta ccggtaaaat
            ....
```

```
26221 gcacaagctg atgagtacga acttatgtac tcattcgttt cggaagagac aggtacgtta 26281 atagttaata gcgtacttct ttttcttgct
ttcgtggtat tcttgctagt tacactagcc 26341 atccttactg cgcttcgatt gtgtgcgtac tgctgcaata ttgttaacgt gagtcttgta 26401
aaaccttctt tttacgttta ctctcgtgtt aaaaatctga attcttctag agttcctgat 26461 cttctggtct aaacgaacta aatattatat tagtttttct
gtttggaact ttaattttag 26521 ccatggcaga ttccaacggt actattaccg ttgaagagct taaaaagctc cttgaacaat 26581 ggaacctagt
aataggtttc ctattcctta catggatttg tcttctacaa tttgcctatg 26641 ccaacaggaa taggttttg tatataatta agtaattttt cctctggctg
ttatggccag 26701 taacttagc ttgttttgtg cttgctgctg tttacagaat aaattggatc accggtggaa 26761 ttgctatcgc aatggcttgt
cttgtaggct tgatgtggct cagctacttc attgcttctt 26821 tcagactgtt tgcgcgtacg cgttccatgt ggtcattcaa tccagaaact aacattcttc
26881 tcaacgtgcc actccatggc actattctga ccagaccgct tctagaaagt gaactcgtaa 26941 tcggagctgt gatccttcgt ggacatcttc
gtattgctgg acaccatcta ggacgctgtg 27001 acatcaagga cctgcctaaa gaaatcactg ttgctacatc acgaacgctt tcttattaca 27061
aattgggagc ttcgcagcgt gtagcaggtg actcaggttt tgctgcataa agtcgctaca 27121 ggattggcaa ctataaatta aacacagacc attccagtag
cagtgacaat attgctttgc 27181 ttgtacagta agtgacaaca gatgtttcat ctcgttgact ttcaggttac tatagcagag 27241 atattactaa
ttattatgag gacttttaaa gtttccattt ggaatcttga ttacatcata 27301 aacctcataa ttaaaaattt atctaagtca ctaactgaga ataaatattc
tcaattagat 27361 gaagagcaac caatggagat tgattaaacg aacatgaaaa ttattctttt cttggcactg 27421 ataacactcg ctacttgtga
gctttatcac taccaagagt gtgttagagg tacaacagta 27481 cttttaaaag aaccttgctc ttctggaaca tacgagggca attccaccatt tcatcctcta
27541 gctgataaca aatttgcact gacttgcttt agcactcaat ttgcttttgc ttgtcctgac 27601 ggcgtaaaac acgtctatca gttacgtgcc
agatcagttt cacctaaact gttcatcaga 27661 caagaggaag ttcaagaact ttactctcca attttttctta ttgttgcggc aatagtgttt 27721
ataacacttt gcttcacact caaaagaaag acagaatgat tgaactttca ttaattgatt 27781 tctatttgtg ctttttagcc tttctgctat tccttgtttt
aattatgctt attatctttt 27841 ggttctcact tgaactgcaa gatcataatg aaacttgtca cgcctaaacg aacatgaaat 27901 ttcttgtttt
cttaggaatc atcacaactg tagctgcatt tcaccaagaa tgtagtttac 27961 agtcatgtac tcaacatcaa ccatatgtag ttgatgaccc gtgtcctatt
cacttctatt 28021 ctaaatggta tattagagta ggagctagaa aatcagcacc tttaattgaa ttgtgcgtgg 28081 atgaggctgg ttctaaaatca
cccattcagt acatcgatat cggtaattat acagtttcct 28141 gtttacctttt tcaattaat tgccaggaac ctaaattggg tagtcttgta gtgcgttgtt
28201 cgttctatga agactttta gagtatcatg acgttcgtgt tgttttagat ttcatctaaa 28261 cgaacaaact aaaatgtctg ataatggacc
ccaaaatcag cgaaatgcac cccgcattac 28321 gtttggtgga ccctcagatt caactggcag taaccagaat ggagaacgca gtgggcgcg 28381
atcaaaacaa cgtcggcccc aaggtttacc caataatact gcgtcttggt tcaccgctct 28441 cactcaacat ggcaaggaag accttaaatt ccctcgagga
caaggcgttc caattaacac 28501 caatagcagt ccagatgacc aaattggcta ctaccgaaga gctaccagac gaattcgtgg 28561 tggtgacggt
aaaatgaaag atctcagtcc aagatggtat ttctactacc taggaactgg 28621 gccagaagct ggacttccct atggtgctaa caaagacggc atcatatggg
ttgcaactga 28681 gggagccttg aataccaccaa aagatcacat tggcacccgc aatcctgcta acaatgctgc 28741 aatcgtgcta caacttcctc
aaggaacaac attgccaaaa ggcttctacg cagaagggac 28801 cagaggcggc agtcaagcct cttctcgttc ctcatcacgt agtcgcaaca gttcaagaaa
28861 ttcaactcca ggcagcagta ggggaacttc tcctgctaga atggctggca atggcggtga 28921 tgctgctctt gctttgctgc tgcttgacag
attgaaccag cttgagagca aaatgtctgg 28981 taaaggccaa caacaacaag gccaaactgt cactaagaaa tctgctgctg aggcttctaa 29041
gaagcctcgg caaaaacgta ctgccactaa agcatacaat gtaacacaag ctttcggcag 29101 acgtggtcca gaacaaaccc aaggaaattt tggggaccag
gaactaatca gacaaggaac 29161 tgattacaaa cattggccgc aaattgcaca atttgccccc agcgcttcag cgttcttcgg 29221 aatgtcgcgc
attggcatgg aagtcacacc ttcgggaacg tggttgacct acacaggtgc 29281 catcaaattg gatgacaaag atccaaattt caaagatcaa gtcattttgc
tgaataagca 29341 tattgacgca tacaaaacat tcccaccaac agagcctaaa aaggacaaaa agaagaaggc 29401 tgatgaaact caagccttac
cgcagagaca gaagaaacag caaactgtga ctcttcttcc 29461 tgctgcagat ttggatgatt tctccaaaca attgcaacaa tccatgagca gtgctgactc
29521 aactcaggcc taaactcatg cagaccacac aaggcagatg ggctatataa acgttttcgc 29581 ttttccgttt acgatatata gtctactctt
gtgcagaatg aattctcgta actacatagc 29641 acaagtagat gtagttaact ttaatctcac atagcaatct ttaatcagtg tgtaacatta 29701
gggaggactt gaaagagcca ccacatttc accgaggcca cgcggagtac gatcgagtgt 29761 acagtgaaca atgctaggga gagctgccta tatggaagag
ccctaatgtg taaaattaat 29821 tttagtagtg ctatccccat gtgattttaa tagcttctta ggagaatgac aaaaaaaaaa 29881 aaaaaaaaaa
aaaaaaaaaa aaa
```

THE END

Index

"S" protein, 117, 118, 119
"S" proteins, 117
1918, 28, 63, 74, 75, 76, 77
1950s, 78, 108
1957, 28, 58, 59, 60, 64, 78
1968, 28, 78
1977 H1N1 human influenza pandemic, 30
1997, 79
2006, 32, 79, 115, 116
2007, 31, 102, 104, 106
2015, 28, 36, 79, 107, 108, 117
2019, 22, 28, 37, 38, 41, 43, 48, 50, 100, 101, 114
21st century, 102
29,881 nucleotide sequence, 119
ACE-2, 10, 11, 117, 118, 119
ACE-2 receptors, 10, 11, 117, 118
aerosol, 14
aerosolized pathogens, 11
AIDS, 6, 10, 28, 74, 102, 106, 113
air raid siren, 100
airborne, 12
Alcohol, 92
American Journal of Public Health, 102, 106
American poultry farmers, 79
Angiotensin-converting enzyme 2 receptors, 10
Anthony Fauci, 68
appointees, 122
Asian, 18, 19, 22, 28, 58, 59, 60, 64, 78, 80
AstroTurf trigger events, 71
Authoritarian, 62
Avian, 59, 78, 102, 108
BAC approach, 116
bacon and eggs, 107
Bacteriophage virus, 113
Bat, 41, 49, 117, 118

benign symptom portrait, 8
Bernays, 107
BGI, 44, 50
bioaerosols, 11, 12
black swan event., 52
Breathing Cycles, 11
Britta Jewell, 7
BSE, 102
bureaucrats, 122
bushmeat, 103
cabin fever, 63
Caixin, 44, 45, 51
CapitalBio Medlab Co. Ltd.,, 50
carbon, 15, 73
cardboard, 13, 14
CDC, 9, 15, 43, 51, 79
Centers for Disease Control, 9, 15, 79
Centers for Disease Control and Prevention, 9, 79
Challenger, Gray & Christmas, 111
Chancoid Haemophilus ducreyi, 10
chickens, 74, 78, 79, 105
Chimp meat, 74
Chimpanzees, 28, 74
China, 5, 13, 18, 28, 36, 39, 42, 43, 44, 45, 47, 48, 49, 50, 54, 55, 74, 78, 102, 106, 114, 115, 118
Chinese Academy of Medical Sciences, 50
Chinese Academy of Sciences, 51
Chinese Communist Party, 47
Chinese government, 37, 54
Chinese Rufous Horseshoe bats, 117
Chlamydia-Chlamydiae, 10
chlorhexidine, 113
clinical psychology, 15
Clorox wipes, 17
common cold, 110, 111
Communist Chinese, 86
Confucius, 102

Coronavirus, 6, 8, 28, 50, 65, 66, 67, 118
Coronaviruses, 10, 33, 41, 47, 49, 115, 117
cough, 10, 12, 15, 21, 38, 113, 122
coup d'état, 70
CoV WIV1, 117
COVID-19, 5, 6, 7, 8, 10, 11, 13, 15, 16, 17, 19, 25, 28, 29, 40, 42, 44, 48, 52, 54, 56, 57, 58, 59, 60, 61, 63, 65, 77, 79, 106, 111, 118, 120, 121, 122, 124
COVID-19 pandemic, 56, 122
CoVs, 10, 32, 40, 41, 43, 47, 49, 115, 117, 118
cows, 74, 103
Creutzfeldt-Jakob disease, 102, 106
Daisy Dukes, 96
Deborah Birx, 68
Deliberative, 9
DNA, 34, 72, 73
Dodger Dogs, 96
Dr. Almazan, 116
<u>Dr. Benatar</u>, 104
Dr. Eckard Wimmer, 31
Dr. Li Wenliang, 45
Dr. Mecher, 66
Dr. Ralph Baric, 36
Dr. Samuel Crumbine, 76
Dr. Shi Zhengli, 47, 48, 49, 51, 117, 119, 123
Dr. Woo-Joo Kim, 17
draconian edicts, 106
Droplet Infections, 11
Ebola, 28, 29
Ebola virus, 29
EcoHealth, 41
Einstein, 102
empirical data, 6, 9, 16
epidemiologic, 14
exponential decay in virus titer, 13
Farmer John, 96, 97
FBI, 17, 30
flu bug, 122
fluid dynamics, 12, 23
fomite transmission, 14

Forensic Profiling, 37
FPA analysis, 48, 49
Frankenstein virus, 73
Frankfurt-1 strain, 116
Franklin, 102
GenBank, 51, 52, 118
Gene sequencing, 50
genomic sequencing, 25, 50
geometric infection rate, 6
geometric infection spread, 6
germ warfare, 30, 31, 35, 42, 114
Germany, 89
Gonorrhea-Neisseria gonorrhoea, 10
Greeting customs, 9
Guangdong, 13, 36, 49, 50, 86
Guangdong, China, 13
Guangzhou, 44, 50
Guro Hospital, 17
H1N1, 28, 29, 30, 75, 79
H1N1 virus, 28, 75
H2N2, 28, 29, 58, 59, 60, 78
H2N2 Avian virus, 59
H3N2, 28, 78
H5N1, 78, 79
half-life of SARS-CoV-2, 14
hand washing, 14, 15, 62, 112, 114
HCoV-229E, 115
HCoV-HKU1, 115
HCoV-HKU1 associated with chronic, 115
HCoV-NL63, 115
HCoV-OC43, 115, 116
HCoVs, 115
hemagglutinin, 78
Hepatitis B, 10
Hepatitis C, 10
herd immunity, 29
HIV, 6, 10, 28, 73, 74, 102, 106
Hong Kong, 18, 28, 78
Huanan market, 39
Huanan Seafood Market, 38
Hubei Provincial Health Commission, 45
Human Factor Analysis, 37
hydrophilic, 15
hydrophobic, 15

Hygienic public health behavior, 11
immunocompromised, 77
in vitro, 8, 116
infectious pathogen, 5, 29, 59
infectious pathogens, 5, 11, 15, 56, 106
intermediate host animal, 117
International Law Commission's 2001 Responsibility of States for Internationally Wrongful Acts, 46
International Nucleotide Sequence Database Collaboration, 118
involuntary behavior, 9
Iowa Beef Packers, 94
Iron Lungs, 32
Japan, 18, 21
JBS USA, 99
Johns Hopkins University, 7, 28
Journal of Virology, 59
Kaiser Health News, 66, 67
Kansas, 74, 75
KF94 respirators, 18
Korea, 17, 18, 22
Korea University, 17
Leonardo, 102
Lincoln, 102
lipids, 15, 73
Liu Dengfeng, 43
Los Angeles County Department of Public Health, 96
Luminol, 122
M.C. Escher, 56
Mark Twain, 90
meat industry, 48, 49, 77, 100
media entertainment complex, 24, 53, 54, 55, 57, 65, 68, 74, 100, 101
MERs, 117
MERS, 10, 18, 28, 115, 116
Mexico, 89
Middle East respiratory syndrome, 115
mirror neurons, 88
Monday morning quarterbacking, 67
Mr. Bungle, 111
Mr. Bungles, 108
mucous membranes, 10, 12

mutations, 26, 36, 40, 73, 77
N-95, 16, 22
N-95 respirators, 16
N-95 Respirators, 16
National Beef Packing Co, 99
National Center for Biotechnology Information, 118
National Health Commission, 43, 45, 51
National Institutes of Health, 118
national security, 72
never let a crisis go to waste, 25
New England Journal of Medicine, 12
New York City, 51, 81
New York State Department of Health, 60
New York Times, 7, 51, 66
Newton, 102
NHC, 45
nominal public health behavior, 5, 11, 19, 78, 106
Nominal public health behavior, 11, 21
North Carolina, 67, 79, 88
nucleotide sequences, 31, 118
on copper, 13, 14
Oppositional disorder, 62
over-the-counter drugs, 111
pandemic, 5, 6, 7, 8, 11, 14, 19, 25, 29, 36, 37, 40, 41, 49, 51, 55, 56, 57, 58, 60, 63, 64, 65, 66, 67, 68, 74, 76, 77, 78, 81, 100, 102, 106, 107, 109, 111, 114, 118, 121, 122
pandemics, 25, 31, 52, 64, 122, 124
Pangolin, 40
Pascal, 102
pathogen aversive, 19
pathogen friendly, 19, 64
patient zero, 6, 42, 118
Pelosi, 54, 55
Pentagon, 32
Peter Navarro, 46
petri dishes, 78, 93
pigs, 74, 78, 79
Pigs, 28, 86, 93, 94, 97
pigs in a blanket, 91, 92
plastic, 13, 14, 114

Poland, 89
polar head, 15
Polio virus, 31
Political theater, 68
politicians, 52, 57, 74, 76, 121, 122
President Trump, 54, 55, 58, 60, 61, 65, 68
primates, 102
propaganda, 109
psychological operations, 92
PSYOP, 91, 107
religion, 124
replicase, 115
Ribonucleic acid, 73
Richard H. Ebright, PhD, 43
RNA, 33, 72, 73, 115, 116, 119
RNA polymerase, 116
roll the dice, 74
Romania, 89
Rufous, 117, 118
Russian Roulette, 72
San Antonio, Texas, 123
SARS, 5, 6, 8, 10, 11, 12, 13, 14, 15, 16, 18, 22, 24, 25, 28, 29, 30, 31, 32, 34, 36, 37, 38, 39, 40, 41, 43, 44, 46, 47, 48, 49, 50, 51, 54, 58, 59, 60, 61, 72, 73, 76, 106, 112, 114, 115, 116, 117, 118, 122, 131
SARS-CoV-2, 5, 6, 8, 10, 11, 12, 13, 14, 15, 16, 22, 24, 25, 29, 30, 32, 34, 36, 37, 38, 39, 40, 41, 43, 44, 47, 48, 49, 50, 51, 54, 58, 59, 60, 61, 72, 73, 76, 106, 112, 115, 117, 118, 122, 131
SARS-CoVs, 117
Seoul, Korea, 17
slaughterhouse workers, 93
slaugtherhouse, 93
Smallpox, 28, 30, 33, 34
Smallpox outbreaks in Great Britain, 30
Smithfield Foods, Inc., 86
sneeze, 10, 12, 15, 21, 22, 23, 113, 122
Soap, 14, 15
Social engineers, 91, 92
social media, 24, 52, 56, 57, 68, 114, 120, 122

South Korea, 17, 21, 22
Speaker of the House, 54, 55
spike (S) protein, 40
Spontaneous utterances, 50
stainless steel, 13, 14
STDs, 9
Stephen Park, 17, 18
stir crazy, 63
Surgeons, 15
Surgical Masks, 16
Syphilis-Treponema pallidium, 10
teaching manners, 108
Tesla, 33, 102
The 1995 Venezuelan equine encephalitis (VEE) outbreak, 31
The 2007 Foot and Mouth (FMD) outbreak in the UK, 31
The Alberta virus project, 34
The Lancet, 37, 38
The State University of New York at Stony Brook, 31
Tonix pharmaceutical, 34
trigger event, 70
Tyson Foods, 99, 101
U.S. Surgeon General, 18
United Kingdom, 89
University of Maryland, 51
University of North Carolina, 36
US Attorney's Office, 17
vaccines, 5, 31, 36, 115
Vernon, California, 94, 96, 97
viral infection, 12
Virology labs, 41
virus replication, 40, 118
virus titer, 13
Vision Medicals, 50
Voltaire, 102
Voluntary, 9
wet markets, 79, 103
WH Group of China, 86
WHO, 8, 13, 18, 44
WIV, 42, 47, 48, 50, 51, 118
WIV1, 117
Wǒ yào nàgè, 79
World Congress of Virology, 123
World Health Organization, 8, 44

World War I, 75
Wuhan, 6, 22, 29, 37, 38, 41, 42, 43, 44, 45, 47, 49, 50, 51, 54, 117
Wuhan Institute of Virology, 41, 42, 43, 51, 117

Wuhan Municipal Health Commission, 50
Wuhan, China, 6, 22, 29, 38, 47, 50, 54
Yulin Dog Meat Festival, 80
Zhong Nanshan, 45
zoonotic, 41, 102

Lightning Source UK Ltd.
Milton Keynes UK
UKHW050144280620
365630UK00007B/107